THE WANDERING

By Trevor B

The wanderer, in every sense a free spirit, stung with visions of past greatness takes up the staff of a modernday pilgrim and will go fifty miles to see a saint's well or a ruined abbey.

Certain illustrations in this book were processed from collotype drawings originally published in Reminiscences of Fen and Mere by J. M. Heathcote 1876

ISBN 0 901680 66 4

PUBLISHED BY TREVOR BEVIS BA, 28 ST. PETER'S ROAD, MARCH, CAMBS. PE15 9NA (Tel: 01354 657286)

Printed by David J. Richards, Printers and Stationers, 1 West Park Street, Chatteris PE16 6AH (Tel: 01354 692947 Fax: 01354 692299)

The wide open spaces seem vast nowadays and rivers, laboriously cut by Scottish and Dutch prisoners-of-war at great risk to health and loss of life, pursue their given course like silver rapiers towards the glowing sunset. Towering above them, sentinels in the form of windmills coaxing water along reed-fringed cuts, sails idling against the three-quarter sky, gave way to modern methods of drainage and no longer grace the Fenland scene.

Foreword

by

PROFESSOR DEREK PORTWOOD, MIDDLESEX UNIVERSITY, LONDON

THE Fens have few of the glamorous and romantic associations of other natural regions of England - the Lakes, the Moors, the Dales, the Malverns and so on. Little memorable poetry and music and drama have sprung from the Fens. It's not that kind of place or at least so I thought in my boyhood in the Fens and before I began to receive each Christmas yet another of Trevor Bevis's slim volumes. The pen and ink drawings were always the greatest delight, followed by the stories and then the detailed information of past and recent heroes and happenings. Eventually it dawned on me that here was scholarship in the making but the stream of volumes, some lightweight, others of considerable substance, made me wonder what sustained this incredible effort. Was it the love of learning usually ascribed to scholars? Having seen this current volume in draft I found out otherwise. Trevor says, 'I learned to love'. These fifty years of dedicated investigation, study and publication are the result of his learning to love the Fens - the struggle between its inhabitants and the forces of nature but above all the spirituality of that relationship expressed in the beauty and wealth of churches created by Fenland communities. Here undoubtedly is the ground of Trevor's abiding love for the Fens and the point where the chronicler becomes the poet.

I suspect that all who like myself have become indebted to him for delighting us with the titbits and treasures of Fenland history and opening our eyes to its natural glories and cruelties will feel privileged to have this glimpse of the soul of this scholar, self described as the wandering Fenman. The skies, stones, earth and waters of the Fens enchant and awe him but his soaring joy lies in the Fenland peoples, living and dead. Leaning on a Fenland bridge, he empathises with prisoners of war in their forced labour. Walking round the streets of his home town, he hears the misery of families stricken with plague. Resting in churches, he communes with worshippers past and present. He revers alike Hereward and the sedge-cutters. Trevor Bevis has learned to laugh and cry with the people of the Fens. Their story has become his own. In this latest volume we learn his love. I know that I will specially treasure the Trevor Bevis volume I receive at Christmas, 1996.

CONTENTS

Chapter One - Coming across the unexpected 1

Chapter Two - Walking through the heart of the Fens 5

Chapter Three - The bank villages: Parsons Drove, Murrow and Guyhirn 20

Chapter Four - Thorney and March: 19th century comparison . . 33

Chapter Five - Whittlesey Mere: the largest freshwater lake in southern England 59

Chapter Six - Stones of the Marsh, sentinels of the Fens 70

In times past churches of marsh and fen vied for prominence with familiar wind engines coaxing water along dykes and discharging it into main drains. Soaring elegantly skywards, finer architectural points enhanced by the sombre flatness, the steeples speak volumes of human faith born of adversity in the face of storm, flood and disaster. The noble tower of St. Botolph's church, Boston, rises like no other from the river bank. It stands upon foundations of great depth, concrete mixed with fleece to give it strength and flexibility against gusting winds. Twenty-five bells, the gift of the people of Boston in the United States of America commemorate the pilgrim fathers, imprisoned during the 17th century in the cells of the English Boston's ancient guildhall.

CHAPTER ONE

Coming across the unexpected

EVER felt like losing yourself . . . ? Feeling an attack of a care-free mood one sunny day I elected to oil the bike - a semi-roadster mountain machine - and pumped pedals eastwards in the direction of the Sixteen Foot river. Why on earth it isn't called its original name beats me. The river or drain however you care to view it once rejoiced in its orginal title, Thurlowe's Drain, after Oliver Cromwell's right-hand man, until some unimaginative nineteenth century bureaucrat decided that it must be the Sixteen Foot. The other great fen drains were changed as well, such as Vermuyden's Drain which became the Forty Foot and Moore's Drain the Twenty Foot. All these were dubbed with the good old English measuring term. None of that foreign rubbish. Hm, I wonder whether the powers that be, sitting in the height of expensive luxury in that palace of a place on the Continent rummaging in their minds to justify their positions will ever get round

to the idea, heaven forbid, that Fenland rivers must adapt to the metric system. It would not surprise me!

Anyway, feet or metric to one side, it's amazing what a simple bit of velocipedic exercise will do for body, mind and soul. To my way of thinking, the Fens were made for two things - tractors and cycles. Tell that to Manea's famous "Flying Eight" - lady landworkers of yesteryear who "have cycles, will go anywhere" picking potatoes, weeding beet, anything you like as long as it's land related. That's if there's any left, bless 'em. It is hard to discern hills; only the medieval islands rise above the level. The Fens still retain the imcomparable sense of freedom beneath the three-quarter sky which gives added light in summertime. The Romans had no idea what they were letting us in for when, sixteen hundred years ago they left to defend their homeland against the Huns. The ancient Brits didn't learn a great deal about maintaining the Roman sea banks in these parts and it wasn't long before the briny crashed through and mixed with the fresh water pouring down from the uplands. That was the start of the Fens before the drainage engines, powered by wind, steam, diesel and electricity sucked the marsh dry. God touched the Fens then with special favour and touches it still. Ah well, what better on a balmy summer day to exercise the limbs then relax beside a drain surrounded by tall grass, reeds and kek with all the little creepy crawlies coming out to inspect the intruder who is far too engrossed in his sarnies and thirst-quenching cans of shandy to pay them much attention.

With nothing particular to do but eat, one allows the eye to roam beyond the far bank. I have never been disappointed in the expectancy that nature will treat me to a special show, often one of drama, perhaps through my own clumsiness in disturbing the grass, damaging spiders' webs and causing momentary panic among those patient, industrious little creatures. Feeling a bit like Robert Bruce of Scotland but without his problems (his wife was imprisoned at Wisbech castle) I watched a spider assess the damage, then it picked up threads and went about creating new strands and joining them up. The humble earwig earns my admiration. A devoted parent, she washes each of her seventy-odd eggs and will repeat the pattern should dirty water soak through the soil and discolour them. I have never seen an earwig fly, yet they can. Almost all their lives they keep their wings folded in hard cases behind the head and rely on toughened bodies, strong legs and sheer determination to get them around the surface which makes an assault course look pathetic.

I soon spotted a promising piece of bank overlooking an open field where I imagined the progress of an old-time binder being pulled by a pair of shires or an old, rusty tractor snortling its way along rows of ripened wheat. It was a scene from yesteryear, but the river and bank were the same as always so I settled myself down quite oblivious to the fact that I was about to be treated to a drama of rare delight. On the opposite side of the river stood a solitary horse chestnut tree beckoning in vain to a clump of similar trees some distance away. This tree hosted a family of crows, mum and dad eyeing with obvious concern the antics of a fledgling barely able to fly, flapping about in the grass beneath the family home. Drama was enhanced. A movement on the far side caught my eye. It was a ginger tom who strolled nonchalantly as only cats can from a rustic fallen down barn. Instinctively I turned my attention to the baby crow which was quite oblivious to mister ginger tom.

It seemed the feline prowler had not seen the stranded bird, but mum and dad had seen him! One flung itself into the air and spiralled down to the fledgling. Hopping around it tried to coax the errant youngster towards the tree trunk. Meanwhile, dad - well, I assumed it was he - emitting raucous caws, hastened clumsily towards the distant trees. What happened next was a revelation. The parent returned accompanied by at least a dozen colleagues, shattering the peace with challenging chorus. To the last crow they alighted in the branches of the host tee. Then they turned and faced the moggy.

Thomas, blissfully unaware of the gravity of the situation (at least he pretended to be) sat his haunches on the grass and indignantly questioned such unruly activity in the tree-tops. Like black clad guardsmen the cawing assembly returned the cat's calculating gaze. In disdain Thomas snatched a quick lick at his tail, then, with head held aloft turned about and stalked away. I pondered that had the cat approached the helpless young crow, the others would have taken off en masse and employed their excavator beaks with excrutiating effect, packing off Thomas in no uncertain terms, minus a few bits of fur and embarrassing loss of dignity. Wisdom of safety of numbers.

Despite this quite unexpected diversion from gastronomic pleasure, interspersed with chortles of unsuppressed mirth, the ham and mustard sarnies went down a treat. Yes! Garnished with countryside relish as well.

Frequently I watch crows and rooks at work in the fields. They fascinate me and I'm convinced these birds are embued with fair degrees of intelligence. Employing sizeable beaks breaking up clods of earth and digging into the ground for tit-bits they are nature's very own JCB's. They seem to have a sense of purpose in life and are admirable clowns in their way, tilting heads cheekily to one side while observing mere men which they have learned to put up with. I admire them if only for the strictness of discipline in tree-top colonies and I know that if one errant crow is so stupid as to break the rules of the game, vengeance can be swift and merciless. At best the culprit becomes an outcast, utterly disowned by the colony – and it's a fair bet there's no going back. Sometimes harsh measures seem necessary, as I witnessed unwillingly a few years back.

I was travelling by car along that stretch of tree-lined road between Coldham and Friday Bridge, to my mind one of the nicest parts of the Fens. Some distance in front of me I could see about fifteen crows forming a circle partly on the grass verge and on the nearside lane. Slowing down I distinctly saw one of the birds dart from the circle towards a crow standing quite still in the centre. It pecked viciously at it and the victim offered no resistance. The forlorn creature had feathers sticking up in all directions and its head drooped submissively.

This was a "court" and execution all in one. The colony was clearly upset and was determined to kill the offender. It was just like a biblical execution by stoning, except that the blows aimed for the defendant were not stones but lethally delivered blows at its back and head. The crows worked to a system, different birds darting from the circle to stab at the victim. It infuriated me and I walked briskly towards them shouting and waving my arms at the same time.

I was astonished that hardly any notice was taken of me as I bore down upon the motley gathering. Eventually two or three executioners turned to look at the intruder, for no doubt that's what I was. Then the group broke up and flapped into the grass, but seeing me almost upon them most, cawing indigantly, took off and landed in the branches scolding me all the time. The victim made no move and rightly or wrongly I scooped it up and carried it to the car where it was deposited in a box in the boot. The sorrowful crow was let out near West Walton. As I drove away it stood by the roadside and I supposed that the unfortunate creature would die anyway. Then again, a miracle may have attended it in its hour of need.

CHAPTER TWO

Walking through the heart of the Fens

CYCLING is great fun, well it is to me. One can see much more than when travelling in a car, even if you are a passenger, and there's nothing like the flowing movement of the breeze in your hair. All right, I know I haven't got much! Rhythmic breathing in time to downward thrusts against the pedals, the tingling of skin as the blood stream sets up a few knots extra. Good stuff! But to really observe the countryside with time to stand and stare, then walking is a must. Using shank's pony is not everyone's idea of an enjoyable and enlightening outing, but some like to be plain old-fashioned and I am one. A summer morning dawned bright with a slight mist hanging over the horizon and it seemed an ideal day for a walk. There and then I decided to walk from March to Ely. Yes! To Ely and why not?

Declaring humbug to all forms of noisy, smelly transportation I hastily planned a route through the heart of the Fens via Welney and Little Downham along the country roads where there would be little traffic. My sole companions? The faithful rucksack filled with nourishment, a camera, notebook and a walking stick. By the time I set out at about 6.30 a.m. a slight breeze had dispersed the mist and the wide open spaces beckoned me along the tree-lined road towards Bedlam Bridge. Half-a-mile to the east, buried beneath the debris of the centuries the Fen Causeway - a Roman road - has its rendezvous with the old course of the River Nene. It comprised of gravel three feet thick, in breadth about sixty feet and extends in length twenty-four miles across the fen from Denver in Norfolk, over the wash to Chalke, thence to March, Plant Water and Eldernell and on to Flag Fen, Peterborough.

This ancient road exemplifies the Romans' indefatigible spirit, but I have no doubt that slaves were forced to make it. As I tramped on, it occurred to me that in the vicinity of the Twenty Foot river

a short distance from the old course of the River Nene, a farmer discovered numerous human skeletons in the fields. Apparently the bones lay in disorder at a junction where the Roman road branched off towards Parsons Drove and Spalding. There was no sign of ritual burial. Were they, I wonder, British slaves brought here and forced to build the causeway until their energy gave out and they were then put to the sword? The Causeway formed a vital link between Brancaster, the Peddars Way and the Roman canal, the Carr Dyke which ran from near Peterborough to Lincoln, a colony for retired Roman soldiers.

Bedlam Bridge, a flat structure replacing the once familiar hump-backed variety gives access to Chatteris and Upwell. Looking over the parapets one commands an unimpeded view of the Sixteen Foot river with its moorhens and visiting swans. As with several fen rivers the road surmounts the bank which serves a dual purpose. Not only does it separate water from the land, it anciently ensured that travellers kept their feet dry. As I walked I noticed an abundance of life. A couple of swans sailed majestically and in places there was a profusion of water lilies with butterflies flitting above them. Turning into a narrow lane leading to Christchurch I perceived for the first time that day the towers of Ely cathedral fifteen miles way floating above the fen.

It was nostalgic to observe in a ruinous farm building an old-fashioned binder rusting away. It brought back memories of the time during school holidays when I stood on a tractor beside my grandfather, towing a binder which nudged ripened wheat onto grating razor-sharp teeth. Nowadays we see and hear dusty, noisy combine harvesters, vastly efficient but impersonal things. Christchurch is a wealthy parish with ample coverage of trees. Akin to an oasis the village is surrounded by treeless fens. A bellringer, I am particularly interested in Christchurch. Here for a time with her parents, lived the famous novelist, Dorothy Sayers, authoress of the Nine Tailors, a bellringing novel set in the Fens. The charming Victorian rectory where the family lived was converted in recent years to a retreat and I can think of no better setting in which to relax from the pressures of modern life.

Miss Sayers was "a bit unladylike" I was told by an elderly Christchurch lady who remembered the family.

"She kept to the fashion of most fen women and wore a 'tater picker's scarf while she was here. She had a peculiar gait and stomped rather than walked."

Dorothy collected newspapers and cigarettes and tinned tobacco from the village shop, for she herself was an avid believer in the weed. The tobacco was for her mother who, I was told, smoked a pipe in the rectory but never outside. What with that and Dorothy's habit of chain smoking the old place must have reeked a bit. Many times her father was

obliged to drive the Morris Minor to the Sixteen Foot bank to collect his daughter who apparently musingly dangled her toes in the water. That wouldn't do for me. Too many pike for my liking.

Miss Sayers never liked the Fens but the drainage system fascinated her as did bellringing although she was never a ringer. A sleuth occupied her heart and she put all three into her famous bellringing mystery which sold worldwide to twenty-eight editions. That book did more for the Fens than any other I know. Eventually Dorothy married and her literary works soon became internationally acclaimed. She and her husband visited her parents at the old rectory occasionally. It was expected of them to attend the village church and the story goes that about five minutes before the service ended, Dorothy's husband discreetly left the church and could be seen hurrying across the fields towards the Dun Cow public house where he contemplated spirits of the other kind! The Sayers' story is Christchurch's only claim to fame. The village was once known as Sulphur Hill. That's strange. There's no hill that I know of and the place which seems to be imbued with an air of peace doesn't look as if it ever had liaison with Old Nick!

I really must continue my walk and headed towards Tips End, even smaller than a hamlet. A homely-looking pub, The Rutland Arms, now sadly gone lured me into its portal. Opposite the entrance a sign indicated the way to Welney and a rustic seat strived to make its presence seen above the tangle of grass and weeds. Mine host would not unlock the door until fifteen minutes had past so I slipped off my rucksack, lowered my posterior onto the bench and proceeded to satisfy the inner man who had taken to rumbling a bit. A little lad of about nine appeared from nowhere and, studying me dubiously, decided to sit down and I asked him his name.

"Stephen", he replied.

"Have a biscuit, Stephen". (In those days it was considered quite in order to offer a child a morsal; how things have changed).

Nibbling the biscuit Stephen began to tell me about his school, and asked me where I was going to.

"I'm going to Ely".

"Coo, that's a long way to walk isn't it?"

I agreed but told him that there comes a time in everyone's life to undertake adventure. Stephen changed the subject and told me he was recovering from mumps. I sympathised with him and said it really was hard luck that he had them in the school holidays, to which he added that he didn't really mind as it was better to have them at his age than an old person, like me!

"You're not really walking to Ely are you? You're too old for that!"

I decided the time was ripe for a drink.

Inside the Rutland Arms, Stephen's mother talked about cameras and we were joined by a middle-aged couple from Chesterfield. They loved the Fens and were at a loss as to why some people thought of them as dreary and uninteresting when there was so much colour, water and limitless sky to behold. I wholeheartedly agreed and excused myself as time was marching on and therefore so must I. Downing the last dregs of a pint cider I bade the small assembly adieu. The winding road led me into Welney, a place of water, much water, and the wash lands.

Like many Fen hamlets and villages Welney consists of a main street sheltered by a huddled and motley arrangement of dwellings, a community hall and a Victorian church. A couple of bridges carry traffic to the winding wash road with its abundance of water loving trees and there's no shortage of that stuff hereabouts. The Old Bedford river has for company a lesser river known as The Delph. About three-quarters-of-a-mile away flows the New Bedford river (they are actually named after the Earl of Bedford who was actively engaged in Fen drainage schemes). Designer of the original scheme, Sir Cornelius Vermuyden viewed the Old Bedford river as the king-pin in his scheme and it was cut during the 1630's. However, it was not enough for the ambitious scheme to work and the New Bedford was cut in 1651. Just think! More than three-hundred-and-fifty years ago where marsh and meres reigned supreme we can now see lush grass stretching to the horizon where the rivers meet the sky. Usually flooded in wintertime, in the summer the washland provides peaceful grazing for cattle, horses and sheep from Earith to Salters Lode, a distance of twenty-one miles.

Whenever necessary, and that's quite often, washlands are allowed to flood, a phenomenon which confounds some people travelling by train on raised tracks above the flooded area and who, in their unfamiliarity with the Fens, think that a terrible disaster has occurred. Protected by wellingtons I have stood alone on a flooded wash pasture completely surrounded by water. And I have seen the aspects witnessed by the Fenland saints of old, watching the sun casting its myriad of sublety changing red and orange hues upon the water - a cascade of colour from the distant horizon to my submerged feet. No wonder the Anglo Saxons called these parts the Holy Land of the English. It's another world with bushes and willows seemingly suspended above the rippling water. The silence says it all. Nature here is in complete harmony, occasionally enhanced by the cry of wild geese winging their way overhead.

I tramped along the New Bedford bank, overlooking what was once malarial and gaseous marsh and visualised prisoners working in white suited gangs, spading out clay and heaping it in high ridges to protect reclaimed land.

Standing in the centre of Suspension Bridge, an ugly iron structure which does nothing to enhance the natural scene, and looking along the length of the New Bedford river is a sobering experience. The waterway forms part of the second scheme of 1651 and the two rivers - Old and and New - work in harmony. The eyes are automatically drawn to the horizon where the silvery waters merge into the overwhelming sky. It is beautiful at all times, in all seasons, and osier and alder are in their element. This is the anglers' paradise and when the evening sun fills the western sky with subdued hues, the medieval fens become a reality in unmatched completeness. The road winding over the wash is quite impassable in times of flood and foolhardy motorists in small vehicles have been known to become stuck between the rivers. Humorous interest abounds when a knowing farmer turns up with a large wheeled tractor and offers to drag failed cars to the safety of higher ground.

I leaned on the parapet contemplating the longest section of the walk and instinctively my mind turned back as it will with historians, to the distant centuries when the New Bedford and other fen drains were being cut. In my imagination I could see dozens of white clad men working in the river bed and on the banks. Standing on the descending bank were rows of labourers holding shovels passing clay from the river bed from one to another. It was placed in carts and barrows and distributed evenly, the very same soil and clay serving its purpose today. A few men paced the ridge armed with chains, surveying instruments and muskets. This was the way the Fens were wrested from primeval nature. Often flawed, it was the stoic efforts of men which finally gave to the nation this land of Goshen. We have to thank foreigners for that and it was the English that brought them here against their will. No self-respecting Fenman whose livelihood would be affected would offer a finger to help.

It occurred to me that the Scots that came to the Fens descended from a race well acquainted with the principles of emigration, the Jewish nation excepted. Scots, like the Jews, are wanderers all over the world and despite the saying that rolling stones gather no moss, with these races that adage is quite to the contrary. "The Scots have a local habitation and a name but, while love of country is ever in their mouths they lose no favourable opportunity of forsaking their country for the most distant parts of either hemisphere".

The men from the bonny highlands that worked in marsh, mere and rivers in the Fens claimed no wealth. They were soldiers defeated in the cause of their beloved country. The making of our highly productive fens is linked with the Battle of Dunbar in 1650 when the whole Scottish army was completely routed by the consummate skill of Oliver Cromwell, himself a man of the Fens. Three thousand Scots were killed and ten

Fen sentinel of old

thousand ended up as prisoners-of-war. The captured men were distributed to several makeshift camps in England and languished in these places at great expense to the English nation.

It soon became clear to several Adventurers engaged in the drainage scheme that here was the opportunity to acquire manpower and successful application made to the government. Supervisors and guards were appointed and in the ensuing months hundreds of Scots were marched from distant places to the Fens. A Corporal Foster was paid a special fee to escort the first group of ill-clothed Scots, a hundred-and-sixty in all, to Earith to commence work on the New Bedford river.

It was deemed necessary to obtain more men in order to expedite the work which proceeded at a slow pace. More prisoners were sent to reception camps south of King's Lynn where work commenced cutting the north end of the river in a southerly direction to meet with that from Earith, altogether involving a distance of twenty-one miles. It was something like the Euro Chunnel but without the complex technology to guide the men using only crude handtools. It must have been dismal working conditions that faced the incoming columns of men who, according to the records were inappropriately attired to face the normally harsh surroundings in a malarial environment where ague was rife. The Scots had to be hale and hearty with no families and they seemed to be large fellows, many pairs of shoes distributed among them being sizes 13 and 14.

Admiral Blake's victory over the Dutch led by Admiral van Tromp who had boasted that he would sweep the English from the high seas and had fixed a broom to his ship to emphasise the point, afforded another opportunity to obtain additional manpower for the gigantic task in hand. This classic sea battle commenced off the Isle of Portland and waged for three days. It ended with the Dutch losing eighteen men-o'-war with the loss of only one English vessel. Thirty Dutch merchantmen were seized and almost forty set on fire plunged to the bottom of the sea. Hundreds of Dutch sailors were sent to prisoner-of-war camps in England. From his eminent position in Parliament John Thurlowe was instrumental in acquiring five hundred Dutch prisoners and an Order was passed to suitably equip them with the necessary tools. Huts were provided for them and other accommodation as thought necessary. These men, with the Scots, were of essential service in forwarding the drainage work and they continued to labour until the Treaty of Peace in 1654, many returning to their native countries. Prisoners were distributed to many places in the Fens, cutting Vermuyden's Drain and Thurlow's Drain for instance; heightening existing banks and repairing them and manning boats for surveyors. The Twenty Foot river near March was surveyed by a Mr. Moore and he had the services of Dutch prisoners to row him and assist in making measurements using a length of chain. Originally the river was named after the surveyor, then it was called The Chain. Some Scotch and Dutch prisoners decided to stay in the Fens and married local women. Their surnames, albeit anglicised, remain to this day in these lowlands.

Many of the prisoners died in harness so to speak, their hearty constitution worn away by the rigours of the task and by the chilling winds which blew unchecked above the great Level. Many fell to the damp climate and the onslaught of malarial related illnesses. It was noted that they worked hard and uncomplainingly but the inhospitable Fen climate took its toll. If a prisoner died he was accorded a proper service and, if convenient, buried in the nearest churchyard. But villages were few and far between and it was usually more expedient to inter a corpse in the river bank. As I stood there musing these things I visualised a little group of men, the prisoners in white Kersey suits and woollen caps, the surveyor and maybe a padre and armed escort, the body in wraps being lowered into the bank it had helped to make. And the chilly fen winds blew and continue to blow over the spot. No monuments were built to honour Vermuyden and the men that helped achieve this great undertaking, unless one sees it in the rivers and drains which radiate to all points of the compass. There should be a monolith to such an achievement seen by critics as impossible and foolish. After all, the debt is entirely ours.

No other walkers did I see that day. My mind traversed the years to the times, not all that long ago, when individuals - the kings of the road sort - could often be seen walking the country lanes. Seventy years ago my grandfather, a devoted Methodist lay preacher, regularly covered fifteen to twenty miles on shank's pony each Sabbath to keep his commitments at fen chapels. Many of these have since closed. The wandering tinker put in a respectable number of miles with pots and pans and an ingenious treadle device on which he sharpened household cutlery, scissors and hedging shears. Like the tramps, he too has gone.

Tramps, well we don't see many nowadays, do we? When I was a schoolboy at Pinchbeck during the school holidays my father occasionally called for me and I accompanied him on his LNER mechanical horse, a type of small lorry with a single wheel at the front. His usual circuit generally lay between Boston and Holbeach and we called at places delivering the goods. On one occasion a large crate was to be delivered to a small monastery. Father jumped out of the cabin and made to manhandle the crate onto the ground.

"Leave it alone, driver", a voice called from an outbuilding. A brown habited monk walked towards us.

"There are a lot of people here who would love to help you with that", he said with relish and walked back to the building.

His voice could be heard bellowing from within. Out came five or six gentlemen of the road at the double, the monk bringing up the rear, ushering them none to gently in our direction.

"Get hold of that crate you lazy good-for-nothings and carry it to the stores".

They did precisely that. They were, said the monk, hobos, bums, tramps, whatever you care to call them.

"They know where their bread is buttered and where to come for it, but by the saints they must earn it! They will eat food fit for a king but work? Not if they can help it!"

Walking along the river bank I spotted two or three rats scavenging for food. They reminded me of an old tail related by an elderly fenman. Apparently late last century a farmer had taken his twelve-year-old grand-daughter to a field where he began tidying sheaves of wheat. Suddenly his sharp eyes noticed a peculiar movement in the opposite field which was divided by a hedge and a little byway. It was as if the soil was heaving up and down. He turned to the child and ordered her to lay upon the ground, to cover her ears and keep very, very still. This she did and her guardian too prostrated himself upon the soil. Before he did so he called out to a tramp who was walking along the track to do the same.

Hundreds of rats were on the run, a phenomenon known as a rat march, the horde of rodents seeking a suitable place to colonise no doubt in order to discover a new source of food. The rats burst from the hedge and in no time at all scampered over the farmer and child who, apparently by keeping still, evaded the interest of the creatures in their hundreds. The couple's eyes were tightly closed but their ears picked up hideous shrieks which went on for minutes. Then silence. The heaving mass of brown fur reached the opposite side of the field and the farmer carefully raised himself, telling the girl to sit still. He approached the tramp and recoiled in horror. The man had ignored his warning and attempted to beat off the rats with his stick. They turned on him like an angry swarm of wasps and as he lashed out at them he fell and was literally gnawed to death. As a result of this terrifying experience the young girl suffered traumatic fits and ended her days in an asylum where in the nineteen thirties she died.

It's surprising what comes into the traveller's mind, especially when alone on the road. Some people in the so-called good old days carried their tools of trade with them and were ready to be hired. These were the time honoured journeymen, engineers, tin smiths and the like who tramped vast distances in search of work. It was the tradition and reached down from medieval times when masons, lead workers, glaziers and wood workers walked the land to enrol for work at the site of a new monastery or church. I recall that one man who lived at Wisbech in the mid nineteenth century, was employed as a bricklayer building the Duke of Bedford's estate cottages at Thorney. The craftsman was known by his colleagues and family as Bob-Down-at-Heel, as he was constantly wearing out his boots tramping back and forth at weekends between Thorney and Wisbech.

I vacated the green bank for the road and the straight way stretched before me more than six miles without a single welcome bend in view. In the distance Ely cathedral softly etched its lines against fleeting clouds and I involuntarily quickened my steps, walking briskly along the pot-holed road and occasionally on the grass to save my feet from spoiling. "Over" Primrose Hill (another hill which is as flat as the proverbial pancake!), the old engine house loomed into sight, a gaunt, empty building dominating the black soil as if it still presaged the future of the level it once drained. Did I imagine the steady thump and hissing of the beam engine in time with its huge scoop wheel lifting the water from the drain and into the river of distant memories? All is still now with the exception of the occasional throb of the diesel unit next door.

The Fens have oft-times by water drowned,
Science a remedy in water found;
The powers of steam, she said, shall be employ'd,
And the destroyer by itself destroyed.

I looked over the black land and marvelled that in these parts, ages ago, marsh and mere mingled and sedge and reeds formed safe havens for herons and moor hens

Thus reads the inscribed stone set into the brickwork. These words embody the past, the present and the future. What did these old bricks perceive? Decades ago they witnessed water filling the dykes and in the uncanny silence of the abandoned engine room are poignant memories to mens efforts to bring fruitfulness to the Fens. Do they perceive, I wonder, the world seas predictably rising against coastlines and eventually reclaiming its old domain in Holland over the sea and in the English Fens?

It was a sobering thought as I looked across the fields lying as they do at sea level and in some fen areas as much as four and nine feet below sea level. Setting a steady gait along the lonely road where even tractors seem to be scarce, I watched for signs of life at Pymore hamlet. Pymore (sometimes spelt Pymoor) has little to show but I was relieved to discover a small general store with a tin roof. To the weary wanderer the sight of it proved a sheer relief and here, perchance, I might obtain a packet of crisps and a gaseous mineral. The woman proprietor asked me where I came from. She stared at me as if I were mad when she realised I had walked from March! A blister was beginning to form on my heel so perhaps she was right. She kept behind the counter and not another word was spoken. So I hit the trail again walking purposely across the black fens towards Little Downham perched alluringly upon its ancient island.

The soil hereabouts is unusually dark and probably the richest in the country. It's the type of soil which makes upland farmers envious. Little Downham and Littleport is renowned for the excellence of celery and the plants develop into crops of the finest quality. I once attended a bellringers' meeting at Littleport and the church ladies put on a marvellous tea for the lads, pride of place given to sticks of celery and, of course, cheese. The celery was locally grown and I complimented the ladies on their expertise and specially mentioned the luscious white sticks. They informed me that the celery was "only grade three". Heaven above knows what the top grade tasted and looked like! Before reaching Little Downham pangs of hunger overcame me and I sat myself on a gnarled bog oak which had been hauled from the soil and deposited at the side of the road.

These old tree stumps lay beneath the surface for many hundreds of years and are a nuisance to farmers who have to remove them before deep ploughing. The stump of my tree was very hard and almost black and I mused how remarkable that this was the oldest seat I had ever sat upon. Many came to light in the 'twenties and 'thirties, ground movement forcing the prostrate stumps closer to the surface. They're not all oaks, most are spruce and ash. It was noted in the early 1800's that a few emerged from the soil and bore the signs of axe marks and one even had the iron axe buried in its bark. Strange it is that the forest as such it seems was torn out of the ground and flung generally in the same direction by the mother of gales.

An astonishing discovery at Wisbech transpired when workers deepening the river struck the bed of a primeval waterway which was hard and stony and, at different distances, covered with silt, seven boats apparently having been overcome by a surge tide centuries ago. Even more astonishing, workmen in the 17th century were resetting stone slabs in the chancel of St. Peter's and St. Paul's church, Wisbech, and digging out soil to a depth of several feet came across an old boat with stones in it and what appeared to be new mown hay.

At Whittlesey, labourers digging eight feet deep discovered perfect soil and swathes of grass lying as if just mown. When the foundation for setting down the sluice at Salters Lode was in the process of being excavated, silt was seen to be ten feet deep. Below that was firm moor three feet thick, and beneath that bluish gault containing the roots of weeds layered along a much firmer and clearer moor substance also three feet thick. Lastly they came upon a whitish clay, probably the original bottom soil.

Amazing stuff, the fen. Sitting on my bog oak I resurrected in my mind a good many unusual discoveries over the centuries in the alluvial fen. Near Connington in old Huntingdonshire a skeleton of a large sea fish nearly twenty feet long and quite petrified was brought to the light of day. At the setting down of Skirbeck sluice near Boston a smith's forge was found sixteen feet deep together with all necessary tools, horseshoes and other things belonging to the smith. At a depth of eighteen feet when erecting a sluice at the mouth of the New Cut near Boston in 1764, roots of trees were discovered standing as they had grown.

I am reminded of the Fens' rich historical past, many artifacts pulled from rivers which were being scoured. These include spears, remains of shields and various swords and daggers found in the Middle Level. When deepening the river at Ely in 1829 a very old sword, in a remarkable state of preservation, was plucked from the silt. Several human bodies have been taken from the fen soil, perhaps the remains of unfortunate travellers lost while attempting to cross the treacherous marsh. Deep down in the fen there is surely a reservoir of artifacts still waiting to be discovered.

I recall a visit to an old fen worthy, a true son of the soil, who lived in a cottage at Upware. He was a retired roder and engine man and possessed a mind filled with anecdotes about Stretham drainage engine. Typical of his kind he was reluctant to say too much about his experiences. Anyone would recognise in him the fen malady if that's the appropriate word, he being cantankerous to a point. The old fellow did admit that over several decades he had found a lot of things while roding dykes. He told me that he kept sackfuls of old rubbish in his shed. I was intrigued and asked if he would show me one.

"Nope", he replied.

Patiently I persisted and told him one or two little stories about the Fens. These seemed to amuse him and eventually he begrudgingly fetched a hessian sack from the shed, spread an old Ely Standard over the table and emptied the contents of the sack. I could scarcely believe what I saw. Before my eyes lay a heap of spear heads, what seemed to be the hilt of a Norman sword, arrow-heads and even rusty pieces of chain mail, one fused to human bone, as well as bits and pieces of pottery. Anxious to obtain the rusting remains of a spear I offered him three pounds. He declined and said he would not give nor sell anything to anyone.

"But what will happen to these things when you're no longer interested?" I asked. The answer was predictable.

"My son will empty the sacks into a ditch".

"Look at it this way", I reasoned. "Professional antiquarians would have a field day studying these things. It all helps to document Fen history and it would be of immense benefit to students".

He looked at me as only a Fenman can.

"These things were taken from the soil and they'll be returned to the soil. I'm not saying any more than that".

I think the biggest find in the Fens occurred at Manea in the mid-nineteenth century. A couple of land workers inspecting a drained piece of fen saw two pieces of timber fifty feet apart protruding twelve inches above the drying soil. They told their employer and he said "leave the field be for two months". Eventually the field had dried out sufficiently to bear another inspection and the two workmen observed that the timbers were much more pronounced and, to their amazement, one was shaped like a horse's head and the other like the tail. They dug between the posts and discovered the sides of an ancient Danish longboat. The farmer, not realising the archaeological significance of such a rare discovery told them to get rid of it. The men dug the timbers out, chopped them up and presented the head to the farmer who had it fixed above the entrance of the farm house. How sad! Manea lost its chance of fame equal to that of the discovery early this century at Sutton Hoo of a great Danish longboat.

While on the subject of Danes, about the year 1900 a March rector, hearing his gardener chopping kindling in the rectory garden, noticed the man wielding an uncommonly large axe.

"Where did you get that axe?" the clergyman asked, antiquarian interests aroused.

"Well, it's like this 'ere, master. I was roding the dyke when the scythe hit something in the grass. It were this axe, so I pulls it out, takes it home. I shone her up, gives her a new edge, made a shaft for it and, bless you sir, she chops like new".

It was a Danish battle axe and one supposes it made a change chopping timber instead of heads!

Now, all this isn't much in keeping with my walk and half-an-hour later I reached the summit of Little Downham (town on a hill). I looked above the vast Fen level, tracing some of the roads I had passed along. It was very pleasant, fields of corn waving merrily in the welcome breeze, contrasting agreeably with splashes of green from sugar beet tops. All hill villages have an intrinsic beauty about them and Little Downham is no exception. The neat little church has an exceptionally fine Norman entrance displaying lots of weird and wonderful carved creatures. I was glad to enter the fane and sat quietly for awhile. And that is not all. The village treasures the remains of a luxurious 15th century ecclesiastical palace centuries ago owned by Bishops of Ely. It looked out over the prelates' watery domain and still retains the original brick oven which baked bread for the august assembly.

Did you know that long ago Little Downham was famous for its stilt walkers? This manner of travelling was commonplace in the Fens and very useful too before the wind and steam engines got to work on the water. At Downham large herds of cattle were put out to feed on nearby harbours or cotes and the men in charge of them were said to be very quick rounding up the cattle and hardly ever falling from their stilts. I abided awhile at Little Downham and managed to find a small cafe where the inevitable cup of tea was welcome. Then came the final trek of the journey to Ely, about three miles, passing on the way a field of cultivated mushrooms. The ship of the Fens, that magnificent grey pile of shaped stones which I had, for most part, in my view from near March, loomed tantalisingly near and eight hours from the commencement of the walk I finally arrived at the Palace Green.

Relieving my back of the rucksack, I sat down on the cool grass, massaged aching limbs and absorbed the intoxicating view of the cathedral's west front, one of the finest to my mind in the land. A Royal Air Force man joined me and we chatted at length about the great church that had beckoned me onwards like a pilgrim of old. He had come to Ely from Norfolk to sample the rare antiquity of the city. He was not disappointed and we bade each other farewell, he to catch a train and me to savour another cup of tea with baked beans and toast and update my notes. I could see the cathedral from the cafe table and my thoughts went back to the time when I climbed the west tower in order to note the inscriptions on the four bells which are housed in niches hewn from the thickness of the walls. The only way to gain access to them was to sit astride ancient beams which brace the tower against the robust Fen winds. Inching myself along them on my bottom, hoping to avoid splinters, I looked down and saw that part of a trapdoor had been left open and I could see the maze marked on the stone floor some ninety feet below. If I had slipped . . . Tension increased when it dawned upon me that one of my wife's ancestors, working on the cathedral tower in the 19th century had fallen and was killed instantly.

There is nothing quite as stimulating as a good walk with the breeze at the rear and the object in view. Not only is it physically good, it is a means of harmonising mind and spirit. Abandon the rat race. Get yourself a pair of boots, a sturdy stick, a pocketable camera (you never known what you'll see), plenty of sarnies and find the discoverer in you. By the way, I didn't walk back. Caught a bus!

CHAPTER THREE

The bank villages - Parsons Drove Murrow and Guyhirn

MANY times I wandered, usually seated upon a cycle saddle, along the length of Murrow Bank. This ridge of raised earth is nowhere as lofty as it used to be and like other defensive barriers in the Fens, built to protect productive land against sea and freshwater floods, the bank carries the road which diminished in height over the centuries. The same can be said of the Roman Bank at Leverington and that between Newton and Tydd St. Mary. The Roman banks formed an integral defence system against seawater incursion and they played a vital, though not always successful, role in these low areas of reclaimed land.

Murrow Bank links three villages, namely Parsons Drove, Murrow and Guyhirn. The road which surmounts it was the only means of communicating with these villages and some distance beyond to Wisbech and March. It was anciently possible to travel from Parsons Drove to Leverington but the way was hazardous and often flooded; Gedney, too, was just about accessible by partly using a protective bank from Clough's Cross towards Crowland. Murrow Bank was very important to parishioners in medieval times, not only assuring them of relatively easy travel but more importantly it protected the east side from threat of fresh water floods.

It is thought that Murrow bank was built in the 14th century by Wisbech's Trinity Guild, a highly efficient religious and practical organisation which performed a very important task in maintaining certain banks in the area thrown up to protect local villages and Wisbech from repeated inundation. It is on record that the prolific Trinity Guild maintained the bank. It was more than familiar with the disastrous consequences of flooding on a large scale and members opinioned that the only way to lessen damage to the considerable acreage between Parsons Drove, Leverington and Wisbech St. Mary was to constantly maintain the bank between Clough's Cross and Guyhirn, effectively dividing the fen, leaving that on the west side more or less to chance and hopefully saving the more prolific fen on the east side of the barrier.

The vast acreage of land and marsh in the direction of Thorney in medieval times was, for best part of the year, a morass and from the 17th century to the mid-18th century could only be sporadically farmed.

One of the main crops was a beautiful green cabbage, not very edible but valuable for oil extraction. It was introduced by the Huguenot and Walloon colonies based on Thorney, Parsons Drove and French Drove. The fen west of Murrow Bank was prolific in sedge and reeds and in the season villagers descended on the fen with scythes to harvest the crops. Small boats of shallow draught were a practical means of transport and when freezing conditions prevailed these could be used like sledges and hauled along frozen waterways and across the meres.

In winter villagers could do little on the cultivated fields protected by Murrow bank and seasonal tasks being temporarily halted by weather conditions harvesting sedge kept them occupied and helped to sustain the local economy. Looking at the fertile land nowadays we tend to take it all for granted. It was a different aspect two hundred and fifty years ago and the work was fraught with dangers to say the least. Murrow bank had to be regularly checked for signs of weakness and repairs effected immediately. Local men involuntarily placed themselves on standby which, of course, was entirely in their interests. Occasionally serious breaches in the bank did occur and the manner of dealing with these was to rebuild the bank similar to a fortress bastion protruding from the west side, placing wicker lengths in the soil to reinforce the repair. Many times in my younger days I wondered why the bank road which is generally straight had a couple of horseshoe bends in it. One has been straightened but the significance of the bends is this: they mark the sites of major breaches in the bank four-and-a-half and three-and-a-half centuries ago, excessive water building up on the west side then forcing

Sedge workers on a frozen dyke

its way through a weak part of the bank. As the water poured into the gap it became wider, as much as two or three hundred yards. The supposedly "safe" level was drowned in some places up to six feet deep and thousands of acres of land disappeared and with it a large part of the local economy, the land not usable for at least two years.

Somehow Murrow, Parsons Drove and Guyhirn managed to survive. It's remarkable how Fen parishes emerged from disaster; stoic determination, the well-known hallmark of Fenmen, won through until the the next time. Hope springs eternal . . . During the 13th century a village near Wisbech succumbed to the sea losing almost a hundred inhabitants, the invading tidal surge causing cottages and farm buildings to collapse, families and livestock drowning. Wisbech, too, was overflowed and the castle suffered great damage.

Dolpoon, a hamlet between Long Sutton and Sutton Bridge was wiped off the face of the earth. Flooding of Marshland and the north Fens makes fascinating study, and it is due to the enterprising souls that lived in these affected parts and who wrestled with the defences and built improved sluices that some sort of order existed at all. The water gate at Clough's Cross and the "four gotes" at Tydd introduced a measure of normality, if that's the right word. Four gotes implies that that number of tidal gates were supposed to act as a safety valve at Tydd Gote, but that area was notorious for periodic inrushes of the sea which spread as far as Parsons Drove, neutralising the usefulness of the water gates. Medieval drainage pipes were discovered beneath the Roman Bank between Leverington and Tydd and by that it is apparent that measures

Sedge harvesters loaded the crop on sledges and boats

were taken to try and drain off the water from the flooded level when it was practical to do so. Now we know what the medieval "gote" means, can I elaborate on Tydd? I can find no reference to this ancient name, except by my own reasoning that it could refer to the tide: "Tide Gate".

I have frequently stopped halfway along Murrow Bank road and wondered how the sluice keeper felt all those years ago when he awoke one morning to realise that he had not secured the water gate the day before. Too late! All night water had poured through the gate and, as a result of the keeper's lapse of memory, much of the level had flooded overnight. I bet his friends, if he had any left, ribbed him over that. The old bank seems higher at Murrow, centuries ago little more than a hamlet. It has a school, a church, a chapel, a public hall and a public house and thereby merits a notch above its former hamlet status. It then comprised a few cottages occupied by fishermen and their families.

What does its name mean? "Mur" seems to have a Celtic root and in almost every place where it applies in the north of England and in Ireland it relates to a beach or a moor. At any rate it implies the proximity of water. The "row" would indicate a line of dwellings, so broadly speaking Murrow can be defined as a row of cottages by the marsh. Not so long ago Murrow had the distinction of being one of two places in the land where the railway lines, owned by different companies actually crossed each other. Furthermore, the village had a couple of stations a quarter of a mile apart, one standing on the Midland and Great Northern line (the muddle and get nowhere line as locals would have it) and the other the famous LNER. Thanks to Mr. Beeching all this vanished into the mists of time. An uncle, Charlie Hart was signalman in the M and GN box and my paternal grandfather operated the LNER box. My father, Fred Bevis, was born at Murrow and my mother, daughter of David Allen, a farmer, lived at Hooks Drove, Murrow, also known as The Alley. So, as you will see, part of my roots are with Murrow, but the same can also be said of Guyhirn and, to a lesser extent, Parsons Drove.

An indication of the hazardous times experienced by the Bank people is recalled in a story which originated in the 19th century. A Murrow resident died and, as was the usual practice, the service and burial was arranged to take place at Parsons Drove. The undertaker wanted to take the horse and cart conveying the coffin and immediate mourners directly across the fields between Murrow and St. John the Baptist church at Parsons Drove, as he considered the bank road to be too dangerous. However, the feoffees controlling the land, refused the request feeling that a precedent would be established and the cortege had no choice but to use the road which in normal conditions was right and proper. Apparently the bank road was like a quagmire and had deep ruts and potholes galore, far worse it seems than the fields. By all accounts the corpse and the mourners had a most uncomfortable journey. It took four hours and those that followed had the unpleasant task of going home the same way by the same means.

As far as place-names go Parsons Drove is self-explanatory. The village developed on a very long fen drove, and for several centuries the community was served by the incumbent of Leverington who had the gauling task of negotiating dangerous droves in winter to minister to his far-flung flock. Eventually a compromise came about and every so often on festive days residents of Parsons Drove, unless they were ill, were under an obligation to make the journey to St. Leonard's church at Leverington. This practice was not uncommon in the Fens. Parsons Drove seems to have its origins from Fitton End, the chapel at that place becoming so ruinous it was considered that St. John the Baptist church would be more convenient for local congregations.

There is every reason to believe that Parsons Drove church originated well before the 15th century which, in architectural terms, much of the building belongs to. The very small south porch which only just protects the door has a badly worn 13th century entrance with typical shafts from that era. Did the older church like that at Fitton End fall to ruin? Guyhirn, too, once had an exquisite 13th century church, or chapel, said to be a gem of a place. I think the harshness of the medieval fens made it very difficult to properly support these little chapels and no parson in his right mind relished the weekly journey to such isolated places. It was difficult to finance their maintainance and so, weary with age and burdened with neglect, the little fen chapels crumbled into the ground. This was especially true after the Dissolution. Increasingly and disturbingly nowadays we see churches declared redundant. Sadly, St. John the Baptist at Parson Drove is one.

A redundant church signifies failure and at best it is turned over to a heritage organisation. It might as well be relegated to the scrap heap. Usually a church becomes redundant for the want of a congregation and that means the financial quota from the parish is no longer possible to raise. In realistic terms many of these churches will be allowed to decay into the ground. I think that St. John the Baptist church was rebuilt in the 15th century by the people for the people. It was the centre of village activities and followed the trend after the Black Death to build new churches and refashion others after the town hall ideal. Here met the village elders, and the sick and dying were admitted for attention. The local guild held ceremonies within the building and it is quite feasible that, like certain other village churches, it was used to store grain after exceptionally good harvests. During the 17th and 18th centuries and in Victorian times onwards churches were used solely for worship.

The old church bears scars from severe flooding which happened in the first half of the 17th century. Either the four "gotes" at Tydd failed or the sea broke through the barrier nearby and water spread out to engulf the Tydds and Newton and Parsons Drove. It caused the chancel foundations to crumble and the east end of the church collapsed. It was impossible to use the building and when drier times returned a temporary wall was erected with the intention of building a new chancel at a later date. The church is still waiting!

I once had a frightening experience in the tower during attempts to copy inscriptions from the five bells. Calling at Southea rectory to obtain the key to St. John's, I let myself in and ascended the tower. First I inspected the bell frame and prodded it with a king size screwdriver to ascertain it would bear my weight. Everything gave the appearance of neglect. Bird droppings almost covered the bells and a musty smell indicated the presence of decay. Having convinced myself that I would be safe I prodded the oak frame, stepping carefully upon it in the direction of a bell next to a louvred window. My heel sank into a piece of rotten wood and I lost my balance, leaning heavily to one side, strik-

The floods engulfed the Tydds, Newton and Parsons Drove, entering churches and houses and destroying peoples livelihood

ing the slatted louvre. A large piece of wood parted company from the opening and fell seventy feet into the churchyard. Fortunately, my shoulder jammed against a transom and I held fast, otherwise I would have followed the broken louvre which was shattered on a headstone far below. Having regained sufficient courage I went about my task, gently sounding the bells which had been cast by Thomas Osborn at Downham Market in the late 18th century. Probably they will never be heard ringing again.

Their music has vanished from this part of the Fens, together with the woad mill, one of five being used at the turn of the century, the others in Lincolnshire. Apart from the forlorn old church and the Victorian edifice at Southea, the village hall and the spanking new Methodist chapel. There are several old farm buildings and at least one 17th century barn, 18th century houses and a couple of pubs - The Swan and The Butcher's Arms. The former mentioned dates at least to the 17th century and was visited by Samuel Pepys who complained that he slept in a cold, damp room and that his journey to Parsons Drove was memorable for the "stinging gnats" which with outsize frogs and the ague were a Fen speciality. Any stranger travelling in the Fens in those hazardous times was fair game and as tasty a morsal for a Fen bred stinging gnat. One supposes it made a change from from the locals!

Gone, too, are the Huguenot and Walloon families that volunteered to live at Parsons Drove in the late 17th and early 18th centuries, though anglicised surnames linger on. Descendants of these families, Markillie (Marquillier) for instance, have descended from people driven from France and the Low Countries and who were persecuted in the name of religion. They all but took over Parsons Drove and their interests were looked after by Mr. Pujolas, a Huguenot pastor, also serving as curate at St. John the Baptist church. The French virtually had the church to themselves and most of the English congregation left because they couldn't understand the language! Pujalos seems to have been sent to this outpost for some mild misdeed, the usual reason being pastors having had the audacity to challenge the French colloque. He drew his meagre stipend from the English churchwardens who farmed church land, but it was discovered that they kept part of the curate's wages for themselves which led to an ecclesiastical enquiry.

Deep in my mind are treasured memories of school holidays in these parts. During the Second World War I spent happy weeks at the family farm at Hooks Drove. David Allen, maternal grandfather, worked a few fields in the vicinity and I recall hot, balmy summer days on the Twenty Acre field sitting in a bone dry ditch at mid-day with grandfather and uncle Wilfred, eating cheese and pickled onion sandwiches washed down with flasks of tea. That was real living!

When the war was raging in Europe I had a passion to flag aircraft. The Fens being flat, the area was ideal for low level flying exercises by RAF and USAF personnel. Out in the fields I would wave my white hankerchief at Mustang and Hurricane fighters and was mainly ignored. Occasionally a 'plane would waggle its wings in recognition. The most rewarding experience in this boyish game happened when riding on the farm tractor towards the M and GN railway line just beyond the field. I could see in the distance a bright flash or two directly above Murrow station. It was the sun reflecting from a twin engined aircraft flying about a couple of hundred feet above the lines. It didn't seem to be going all that fast, and I hastily pulled out my handky and began waving it. As the 'plane drew near, grandfather and I could clearly see the pilot and co-pilot looking in our direction and one put up his arm and waved. Then we both saw the black cross on the fuselage and realised it was a German aircraft, probably on a reconnaissance flight. Occasionally enemy pilots flying from the Wash, picked out rivers and railway lines and followed them towards towns and cities.

David Allen was not amused.

"You silly little beggar!" he shouted, glancing reprehensively at me. "You could have got us shot to pieces".

A Methodist lay preacher, my grandfather was keenly interested in the Alley chapel near the farm. All the family attended its opening in the mid 1920's and despite many of the little fen chapels having closed in recent years, the little Alley chapel soldiers on. Its foundations are stiffened by railway lines forming a raft to ensure that the shrinking peat will not affect the walls.

My family links with these parts extend to Guyhirn, a one-sided village dwarfed by the lofty banks of the river Nene. The Culy's lived here and the family can be traced in the Fens for over three hundred years. Great-grandfather Culy was a little, rotund man of mild manner. He lived in a cottage opposite the river and worked as a lengthman for the LNER between Guyhirn and French Drove, supplementing his meagre wage as a cobbler in his spare time. There were several children and as was often the case in those days the family were hard put to manage. He had a strong faith and he loved to relate the story of the time he was working on the line, worried sick about his youngest daughter, my grandmother, a frail child.

"There was no food in the larder that morning", he would say, "and I was worried about Patsy especially. So I knelt down beside the rails and prayed to the Lord that we all might have enough to eat that evening.

"The Lord heard, and bless me a few minutes later, if a cock pheasant didn't get itself caught in the telegraph line, broke its neck and fell at my feet. Patsy enjoyed her food that night".

Anciently defined, the place-name Guyhirn means "the corner of the salt-water ditch". The ditch was long since overcome by the tidal river, once known as Smith's Leam, which was straightened here and there and deepened over the last two hundred years to render it navigable between Wisbech and Peterborough. Among its old-time traffic was a regular picket boat carrying passengers and goods between the two places and, during the Napoleonic wars, vessels carried dejected sons of la belle France into years of captivity at Norman Cross prison.

The demands of the twentieth century fixed Guyhirn into a corner, traffic on the A47 no longer passing through the village, but diverted onto a new stretch of road which one supposes acts as a kind of bypass. It effectively removed the old, narrow and hazardous bridge built when horse traffic was the norm, but the sparse number of traders in the village miss the benefits especially of holiday traffic passing through.

Guyhirn was the site of an ecclesiastical experiment in the 15th century at the time when serious thoughts were developing as to the feasibility of draining large tracts of marsh and converting it into farmland. The enterprising, talented Bishop Morton of Ely took a great interest in surveying the Fens and reasoned that a new leam from Guyhirn to Stanground would not be amiss. This, he thought, would serve a two-fold purpose. Initially the leam would help to drain the marshes between Whittlesey, March and Wisbech and at the same time

The Puritan chapel at Guyhirn, one of two in existence

the excess water could be directed into the main river and assist in improved navigation to Wisbech port. The leam which is named after the bishop came into being about 1470 and was linked to a lagoon which collected water when the tide was in, then when the tide ran out the water of the lagoon discharged with such force as to create a turbulence along the river bed, in effect scouring it all the way to Wisbech and beyond. Well that's how it was supposed to work.

The idea failed on a few unconsidered points, the prelate having had the leam excavated insufficiently wide enough nor deep enough. It did in fact collect water in its best hours but in winter was inclined to discharge it into the marsh, causing floods as far away as the old course of the River Nene between Benwick and March. The farming community between Morton's Leam and Whittlesey did not help matters and took advantage of the shallow depth, dropping stones and gravel on the bed in order to facilitate a better crossing. Bishop Morton erected a wooden tower at Guyhirn not far from where the railway station used to be that he might reasonably survey the progress of the leam some distance towards Stanground. I remember some years ago seeing huge stone slabs close to where the leam joins the river and it would not surprise me if these formed the foundations for the bishop's tower. From here he must have often looked over the village with its beautiful 13th century chapel before neglect caused it to tumble down. Today Guyhirn keeps itself afloat with a pub or two, a Victorian pseudo-Gothic church, a school, a public hall and a few commercial premises. It also has a rarity as well as a very intriguing story from the past.

The rarity happens to be the little Puritan chapel on the way to Tholomas Drove. Simply and austerely constructed at the end of the Commonwealth era, this plain but significant building beautifully exemplifies the attitudes of the founders and congregations that originally sat in its uncomfortable pews, so close together as to prevent anyone from kneeling. Hatpegs on the wall to accommodate the long, pointed Puritan headwear, and the fitting scarcity of aids to worship found in most other churches transform this little gem of a place into a Tardis - a real time machine. The atmosphere really does conjure up the high-hatted gentlemen of sombre visage accompanied by their wives and daughters with stiff starched collars and plain attire. The perfect folk of Oliver Cromwell. They frowned when lambs frollicked on the Sabbath and every day their duties were measured in the usefulness of what they did for the Lord. In some ways they may well have been right and it all comes streaming through the centuries in Guyhirn's evocative little chapel. It was built in 1660 and was given a bell which may have been the one which called the Huguenots to prayer in the village of Sandtoft in Hatfield Chase, far north. Sad to relate, the little church at Sandtoft

- the spiritual home of persecuted Huguenots and Walloons - was burned to the ground by the native fishermen of Hatfield Chase who resented their rights being threatened when the fen was being drained by "foreign families". The fishermen and wildfowlers attacked their homes, destroyed sluices and set fire to wheat crops and all this eventually resulted in an exodus from the area. The French speaking families trekked to Thorney and were given every encouragement to settle in that vicinity by the Earl of Bedford who owned large areas of marsh and land formerly the estate of Thorney abbots. The establishment of the colony and its branches at other places in that part of the undrained Fens introduced a new chapter in the history of Thorney and especially at Guyhirn.

The Culy family settled at Guyhirn about 1670, preferring to live there it is thought rather than at Thorney. Undoubtedly members of the family which the writer himself is related to, strongly resented being connected in any way to the established Church. At Thorney the bishop of Ely had kindly consented to the Huguenot colonists using the abbey church for services, but the Culy's somehow linked the Church of England to the Roman Catholic Church by which their family and thousands of others like them had suffered so terribly on the Continent.

Then, Guyhirn was not far removed from other fen outposts, regarded by some as dens of iniquity, made unwholesome perhaps by inward looking tendencies and intermarriage which is usually the resort of isolated communities restricted in travel. This may have been the spur behind one member of the Culy family who nurtured a deep yearning to convert the inhabitants to a new spiritual beginning. In his mind he saw Guyhirn as the seat of his own diocese and he used the tool of dissension and unbounded enthusiasm to further his desire. David Culy founded the Culimites and here, at Guyhirn, he nutured the sect and progressively involved its expansion to other places.

He was first inspired at a meeting at Christ Church, March led by Reverend Francis Holcroft who had a very extensive circuit in Cambridgeshire. Warming to the cause, Culy began attending Baptist meetings at Green Street, Cambridge. He felt no satisfaction however until his association with the Independent Chapel at Rothwell, Northants which he first visited in 1691 and became a member. Later, other members of the Culy family and friends joined the congregation at Rothwell. "The Church in the Fens" was frequently mentioned in the Rothwell church book, many of its members descended from Huguenot and Walloon families living at Guyhirn and places nearby. Culy was noted as an excellent speaker and on September 12th, 1691 at Rothwell after refreshments he entered the pulpit and preached. The enthusiasm of those early days was such that meetings could go on night and day and sermons might well last two or three hours. The orator within him really shone after he had met Pastor Richard Davis, an itinerant preacher who did much good work at Rothwell. Culy adopted the style of Holcroft and Davis and he, too, became a preacher of the road. He was very successful "and went on to do good work in Cambridgeshire" where one of his principal foundations was the existing Baptist church at Pound Lane, Isleham. *(Memorials of the Independent Chapel at Rothwell: G. T. Streather).*

Initially the church at Guyhirn was linked to the mother church at Rothwell but it was Culy's intention that the Guyhirn church be an independent one and that was approved by the meeting at Rothwell. Culy's success and style as a preacher earned him the title of Pastor, but occasionally he stepped over himself and while a member of the Rothwell congregation was accused of using unsound expressions and preaching errors of doctrine. His powers of oratory stood by him and he successfully answered his critics and was restored to full membership.

Culy's shortcoming was his lack of tolerence of local clergy aligned to the Church of England and he would frequently dispute with them. For this he was summoned to Wisbech Assizes in 1694 but happily acquitted. However someone (believed to be the Bishop of Ely) had other plans. Culy was informed that it might pay dividends to introduce his mission to King's Lynn and on entering the town he was seized by a naval press gang, put on a tender and whisked away to the North Sea. Undaunted, Culy decided to use a secret weapon! Evidently he had a fog-horn of a voice and he put it to good use, continually praising his Saviour. At first the hard-boiled sailors, hardly ripe for conversion, ridiculed him and went out of their way to make life hard for him. However, Culy persisted, turned up his voice and sang like he had never sung before! Hymns issued from his lips loudly and incessantly. It was too much for the crew and the men pleaded with the captain to get rid of him and he was put into a boat and rowed ashore off Yarmouth Roads. Culy made his way home preaching on the way, of course. Eventually he reached the Isle of Ely and friends made him a land owner at Ring's End,

and this assured he would never be deported. Having survived Wisbech Assizes and the pressgang, Culy proceeded to establish more churches in the Isle of Ely, one right in the bishop's backyard so to speak, at Isleham. It was at Isleham to the bishop's delight that David Culy blotted his copybook and the progress of the Culimites temporarily halted. A married man with a family, Culy had an affair with a woman of Southery and fathered an illegitimate child. The church elders at Isleham had no choice but to eject him and the woman from the fellowship and Culy returned to Guyhirn where, for a season he kept a low profile. Culy's sect existed for a hundred-and-fifty years and enjoyed a total membership in the ancient Isle of Ely of nine-hundred souls. In 1693 there were twenty-two brethren and eighteen sisters in the Culimite church at Guyhirn, but in 1755 only fifteen families remained loyal to the sect. It soldiered on and David's son, Isaac, was granted a licence for an independent meeting house at Wisbech. The spark finally went out in 1852, the last few members gathering in "a small, mean building at Walsoken".

In its heyday members represented Elm, Beadlinghay, Thetford, Soham, Whittlesey, March, Allerton, Upwell, Tholomas Drove, Wisbech and Isleham. Soon after he had left Isleham fellowship Culy was busy preaching at Billinghay, Lincolnshire where, not surprisingly, he challenged the vicar to dispute with him at the village cross. The clergyman declined but had the last word when David Culy died. He allowed his body the doubtful privilege of being buried in an obscure corner of the churchyard without being recorded in the parish church register, the usual procedure with nonconformists.

The Culimite church at Guyhirn was not without its problems, the Rothwell fellowship occasionally querying unsuitable expressions. A female member of the Guyhirn congregation was visited and admonished "for marrying a carnal man" and other members admonished for practising unsuitable ways. Culy's eloquence extended to his pen and he wrote diverse papers and published substantial religious works. He wrote about sixty hymns typical of the period, and a handwritten copy is kept at the Wisbech and Fenland Museum. In endless motion the muddy waters of the River Nene surge inland and seawards on the tide bearing distant memories of an extraordinary man - the Bishop of Guyhirn.

Thorney abbey overlooked "a paradise of fruit trees and vines"

CHAPTER FOUR

Thorney & March - 19th century comparison

I HAVE lost myself in Thorney on many occasions and been glad of it. It is the wanderlust in me that brings me to this place and I can never get my fill of rare sights, be it hand carved detail within and without the abbey church or treatment of stonework on the fine houses opposite The Green, regular and irregular rooftops and the trees with which Thorney is blessed as indeed are those that live there. Anyone residing in the symmetrically built estate cottages just off the notorious A47 unreasonably burdened with traffic may think of Thorney differently, but those with homes south of the abbey live in a different world.

History really is vibrant at Thorney and there can be few places that cherish a past dating to the Celts, a few settling at Ancarig, as Thorney was called, more than a thousand years ago. Then, it was a seemingly God forsaken place with an abundance of wild briars or thorns from which it was later renamed. God came here in the form of three tired hermits, tired that is of monastic life, determined that they discover themselves in their own time, free from disciplined ritual. They were Celts, Tancred, Torcred and their sister Tona and at Thorney they realised their ambitions to live as anchorites. Fourteen centuries hence is a long time yet a contemplative spirit can still sense a presence bequeathed to the village from those quiet days when the hand of God worked through chosen vessels and later His saints.

It doesn't take long, even for the first-time visitor to realise that Thorney occupies a treasured place in architecturally-tuned minds. Even the traffic's on-going roar cannot mar the charming evidence of a rich past seen in the rows of terraced cottages with fine entrances, leaded windows and manor-type chimney stacks, perfectly complementing the massive, elegant brick tower overlooking Crowland Road. Thorney gives the lie to the Fens and the beauty and style so evident here seems more enhanced because, believe it or not, this assuredly is the Fens. Yet it would certainly not be out of keeping were it planted in the Cotswolds. Lower the eyes on bowers of greenery, the gabled houses in profusion. The Green where abbots and monks were wont to walk, and why not? After all, it is holy ground. Formerly an oasis surrounded by marsh,

The abbey's ancient turrets overlook a pastoral scene at Thorney

Thorney witnessed a mighty struggle for more than a thousand years for its place in the Fens involving the Church and marauding Scandinavians who set fire to the abbey. Then there were Fenmen and foreigners, the former trying to retain their birthright as fishers and wildfowlers and the latter gainfully employed to change it all, even nature herself.

Thorney cherishes a powerful and evocative history stretching back almost fifteen hundred years when the Fens proved irresistible to the saints elect. Many of the small and larger malarial islands attracted the holy recluse to pursue and develop their calling. It was no coincidence that at Crowland, five miles distant, Guthlac, a man of military and religious instincts chose to set down his roots in a place, then, if anything, more forsaken and depressing than Thorney and that the great English patriot, Hereward the Wake chose to be buried near his wife at Crowland. Crowland and Thorney shared the doubtful distinction of utter desolation, both places liberally covered with wild briars and more than generous amounts of obnoxious oozing mud ("cru") from which Crowland is said to derive its name. Guthlac's bones rest at this spot, and at Thorney the dust of Tancred, Torcred and Tona their sister, remembered for their renunciation of the world, sleep as canonised

The bones of St. Guthlac and Hereward slumber at Crowland abbey

saints. Although anciently rivals Thorney keeps a link with Crowland. Guthlac, searching for a place in the Fens, came to Thorney and met Tatwin the boatman; it was he who conveyed Guthlac to Crowland. Tatwin is commemorated on the west front of Thorney abbey.

Compared with Thorney I think of Crowland as a grey town of renown. Both places have an abundance of solid grey buildings but the environment surrounding Thorney seeps from every nook and cranny rooted in every age that gave it fame. Walking down the road towards Crowland abbey one sees tired buildings, grey to be sure to match the famous church with its handsome if ruined west front with tiers of tired figures depicting saints and kings. The old bridge, a curious site at a dry junction, has three stepped entrances and is probably unique. Several

Abbots and kings passed over Crowland's 14th century bridge

old towns boast a stone cross but not Crowland. The town is distinguished for its abbey and the bridge which they say has a figure of Christ (or could it be a carving from the abbey?) very worn. It's difficult to tell which is the more popular with tourists. The elderly of Crowland used to gather at the bridge and gossip about all manner of things. It was known as Bridge Talk, so I reckon this ancient structure could tell a juicy tale or two.

Crowland was the place of the skull. It isn't now more's the pity. I recall the time when standing beneath the abbey tower with five bellringers ringing a bell less than a couple of feet away from the baleful glare of an early abbot's skull contemplating my posterior. The skull used to be enclosed in a glass sided box on the wall until a mindless person stole it. The aged cranium sported a king-size cut made by a sword thrust. It captured the imagination of people entering the abbey for the first time, but why on earth display somebody's cranium to all and sundry when it would be deemed an act of dignity and respect to bury it in the ground outside?

A briar marks the spot where, beneath the grass, the floor of St. Guthlac's cell was discovered in modern times. That man certainly started something at Crowland fourteen hundred years ago. What a forlorn and desolate place it must have been for him to meditate, surrounded by marsh, fogs, briars and, according to him, all manner of devils to make life intolerable - maybe those of the human kind! When Guthlac died, worn out by the rigours of the place I imagine, he was buried at Crowland and a friend of his, a King, founded the abbey in his memory.

A traditional scene of sedge harvesters with sickles and sledges

There's quite a lot of wash land near Thorney and Crowland as well as dykes and drains for good measure. A hundred-and-fifty years ago when Jack Frost touched the land and marsh turning it into slivers and lakes of reflective ice the boys and girls of the towns and some adults, too, made capital of the season turning out on skates trying to avoid the workers who took advantage of the chilly season and pulled sledges filled with sedge. The dykes and drains were useful too and traditional fen lighters sailed pre-arranged distances conveying reeds used for thatching buildings. I picture the scene when the mood directs me to Wicken Fen, alas the only part of real fen remaining in these parts.

I cannot quite make up my mind whether Thorney is a village or town. Some recognised it as a town a century and a half ago by reason of its railway station, gas works and large sheep market. There's nothing like that now. Ancarig (Thorney) existed in the 7th century and it was set ablaze by marauding Scandinavians who sailed the Fens leaving their firebrand visiting cards at several monasteries. Then along came Hereward the Wake and he used the island as a fastness against the

Fen lighters were used for carrying reeds for stacking

Normans. After a year-long siege of the Isle of Ely the Normans demolished Thorney's Saxon abbey and replaced it with one in the familiar Romansque style of which part of the impressive nave remains. William of Malmesbury, writing in the 13th century declared that Thorney was a paradise, the industrious monks in their courage and piety turning the marsh into fruitful fields, vineyards and orchards. It must have been a wonderfully solitary place for the monks, and many abbots of this mitred abbey were outstanding scholars and authors of their times.

Little is left of the abbey but the fragments we see are noble enough to build up our imagination of its former glory. There is more Norman work at Thorney than is seen at Crowland which has a delicate dog-toothed arch open to the elements, the church itself mainly from the 15th century. Both monasteries were severely mutilated at the Dissolution but Thorney was saved from total destruc- truction in 1638, much of the squared stone having been taken to Cambridge for the construction of Corpus Christi college and also to villages and towns in the Fens where it was used in the restora- tion of churches and building of cottages and farms. Thorney abbey church was

The Norman nave of Thorney Abbey. T.A. Bevis

a very large complex, but now it is merely a fraction of what it used to be. Looking at it now it's hard to realise that the abbey was three hundred feet long, with six aisles and western towers and spires. The stone which made up the monastery can be seen in the old houses opposite The Green and in the large house which served as the abbot's residence. How many monks I wonder lay beneath the streets in the vicinity? A stone coffin was found some years ago. The bones of these men are in the place which nurtured solace and learning, music and prayer, industry and charity. They were more fortunate than the last novices and monks who, with the abbot were pensioned off and sent away. When the abbey doors were locked for the final time another stirring chapter in the annals of history at Thorney came to an end.

I feel at home near the remains of this evocative building for it was in Church Street nearby that a few of my ancestors lived at the turn of the century. Their residence was a charming cottage dating to the 1720's - the place with the blue shutters. It's a coincidence that this particular abode enchants me for within it lived the late Hugh Cave with his wife, Renate. This kindly man was a mine of information about the district and to sit here with a cup of tea and biscuits to hand and listen to him was a revelation to me concerning working attitudes of past generations. Years ago my grandfather and my mother, then a teenager, called at the house with the blue shutters and left punnets of strawberries.

After the Benedictine abbey had been dissolved the Earl of Bedford, a member of the illustrious Russell family, acquired the Thorney estate, an act which set the village on course to a series of remarkable events. Previously the abbot and monks had achieved limited miracles in crop production and to do that it was necessary to drain the lower levels of the island. The monks dug a ring ditch at the upper level, then connected it with a lower ditch a few feet above the level of the marsh. This collected the water from the upper level and discharged it into the marsh thereby allowing the land in between to be cultivated and grow crops. The former marsh adjacent to the lower ditch became reasonably dry in the summer months and lush grass grew on uncultivated areas very suitable for feeding stock. This form of drainage was entirely local and I have no doubt that the monks derived much satisfaction from experimenting with husbandry and self supportive means.

Thorney estate was considerable and a survey in 1574 shows 240 acres of upland ground, 160 acres timber which included a thousand oaks worth £500. There were 16,000 acres of fen, and reeds and willows growing on it were valued at £200. Buildings attached to the abbey were valued at £1,000. Brown Willis wrote that the monastery precincts were surrounded by a moat twenty feet broad and a mile long - this probably the upper ditch to keep the adjacent area dry - and the precincts

St. Kenulph's cross

comprised forty acres. The monastery boundary extended halfway in the marsh between Thorney and Crowland. Abbots at the latter place were very particular about marking the boundary between the two monasteries. Among the several crosses erected was one known as Kenulph's Cross and should a Thorney monk trespass beyond that without prior permission he was in trouble! This cross was moved in recent times and stands in a farmyard - quite the wrong place - a few hundred yards away from its original site beside the road.

Francis, fourth Earl of Bedford, harboured a great dcsire to drain the Fens. He followed in the footsteps of Robert Tipper and John Gason who, in 1626, made studies for a similar project. The Earl was backed by Charles the First, and Sir Cornelius Vermuyden the eminent Dutch land drainage engineer was commissioned to prepare a plan which was partly financed by a group of Gentlemen Adventurers. Vermuyden had had considerable success at embanking the Thames at Dagenham and had gained first hand experience in designing the ill-fated scheme to drain a smaller area of Fen at Hatfield Chase near Doncaster. I have already mentioned the misfortunes of the Huguenot and Walloon colonists while

attempting to drain Hatfield Chase, Yorkshire. The English living there would have nothing of it and the colonists were obliged to leave, all their hard work having come to nothing. Many of the refugees had heard of the scheme to drain the Cambridgeshire Fens and Vermuyden, conversant with their skills in this field spoke favourably for them. The Earl of Bedford, anxious to procur labourers for the task in hand and unable to gain support from the Fen natives, encouraged the French-speaking people to live on his estate in and around Thorney.

The persecuted families enriched Thorney beyond comprehension. Their indefatigible labour in difficult and hazardous terrain, upstanding and respected attitudes and sincerity in matters of religion, earned them the gratitudc of the nation albeit after many years had elapsed. The debt is entirely ours. Not only did they inject expertise into the scheme they later hired and purchased land from the Earl, producing excellent crops on former marsh ground. One of their specialities was colza, a sort of inedible cabbage which covered the ground in great abundance with a beautiful green colour. It was grown to extract oil said to be ideal for softening wool and to fuel lamps.

Mindful of their traumatic experiences in Yorkshire,. the settlers tended to live away from the village, probably to minimise the risk of upsetting people averse to the drainage scheme. The Bishop of Ely granted them use of the abbey church for services conducted in the French tongue. Highly skilled Huguenots and Walloons attracted to England introduced new methods in many trades, particularly that of producing woven material. Those living in the Fens are not credited with belonging to weaving communities but there was probably a connection - if only from selling colza oil - with communities in East Anglia involved with the weaving trade. The Huguenots introduced the French paring plough to the fields surrounding Thorney. This was a light implement cutting a few inches into the top soil. Deposits of peat were heaped up and set on fire, ashes then distributed over the land. From this practice developed the controversial custom of burning stubble, discontinued in recent years. Quite often the practice of burning pared earth caused smouldering beneath the surface which spread considerable distances. It was a problem in these parts, the underlying peat easily ignited. Even tracks and highways were set alight by careless people emptying pipes, for instance, and a law was passed forbidding people from smoking while travelling along local roads.

The strangers, as they were known locally, worked equally hard to preserve the fields from flooding, a not uncommon occurrence in the Fens. Thorney and neighbouring fen were frequently washed by water flowing from breached embankments on the south of the village and also by excessive water from the direction of Wansford which mixed with that overflowing from the River Welland running close by Crowland. The floods spread out, in particular eastwards to Murrow Bank, sometimes breaching it. In winter, Thorney inhabitants and colonists patrolled in groups along river banks between Whittlesey and Thorney, placing gauges in the earth at water level. These tell-tale markers indicated sudden drops in the water level and that somewhere along the bank a breach had occurred and water was pouring through it onto the land. Observers mounted horses and raced off to warn village residents and outlying farmers of impending disaster. Parties went to the breach with shovels and open framework of woven strips of cane which was worked into the ruptured bank and earth heaped onto it. When colza and wheat crops were not being harvested Thorney inhabitants and colonists came together and employed their skills in a harvest of a different kind. They went out to the fringes of remaining wetland and cut and gathered sedge which could grow up to fifteen feet in height.

I can sense the foreign presence in and around Thorney abbey. Inside the building floor slabs are inscribed with French names and several old headstones in the churchyard indicate the final resting places of "strangers" that lived in and around the village. This chapter in Thorney's long history is mirrored in a tablet on the wall inside the church, honouring the memory of the first of five French pastors. Ezekiel Danois of Compiègne in France was banished from his homeland and came to Thorney to look after his flock who, like him, had suffered persecution for their faith. In a way this man was a worthy successor to Thorney's saints and the inscription in French tells us "in unwearied zeal, learning and strictness of life he was second to none; a great treasure of literature was here hidden from the world, known to God and himself, few besides". Pastor Danois died at Thorney in 1674, the last pastor ending his ministry here in 1715. The Huguenot and Walloon colony practically ceased to exist after 1726 but its memory lingers to this day in the names of several families living in the Fens and elsewhere. In terms of religious zeal, moral and disciplinary example, achievement in the marsh and in the fields, in defensive works against floods and dogged determination to succeed in the face of disaster and adversity, this chapter of history at Thorney is without equal. It was a miracle of sorts but a greater miracle in the social sense was yet to come.

In the years following the Dissolution of the Monasteries, land owners of manorial status acquired vast estates formerly belonging to suppressed religious houses. Sir William Russell obtained a royal grant of the entire lordship of Thorney, and Francis fourth Earl of Bedford procurred the right of a market at the village. This elapsed in 1830. The market was probably held on The Green which was known as Market Hill. It was renewed by Wriothesley, Second Duke of Bedford in 1716 and fairs for horses and cattle continued for several years. Large flocks of sheep were raised at Thorney and thousands sent to Smithfield Market. By the middle of the 19th century Thorney had taken on the aspect of a small town and had a railway station, a gasworks and other amenities not normally associated with small communities, certainly in the Fens. The horse fairs took place in Station Road and the annual feast continued up to the advent of the Second World War.

The involvement of the Earls and later Dukes of Bedford was of particular benefit to Thorney and one supposes that were it not for the establishment of the great abbey the village would be no different from any other place in the Fens. Members of the House of Russell frequently visited the estate between 1727 and 1729, and it was said that had not Wriothesley died prematurely it was his intention to build a palacial residence at Thorney for himself and his descendants. Unfortunately this was not to be and the family house was built at Woburn instead. It was left to another member to nurture his skills and interest with Thorney and its huge estate in mind and in all events eventual developments more than made up for the omission of the house.

In the fourth decade of the 19th century the Duke of Bedford resolved to evolve his Fen estate on productive and experimental lines.

Villagers cut and gathered sedge which grew fifteen feet in height

The magnitude of his vision and the sheer magnificence of it brought fame and recognition to Thorney and bequeathed a priceless heritage exemplified in the opulence of Victorian elegance and practicality. When walking in the village, to the right and left one sees an unusual blend of architectural styles ranging from romansque Norman and refined Tudor to dignified aspects of the Jacobean and Victorian eras. Of the latter style it is written of Thorney: "There is no village in England with a more extensive display of well designed Victorian cottage architecture". Much of this is the work of Samuel Teulon of Huguenot descent, who left his mark at many places in the country.

The major development at Thorney in the mid 1800's centred on the transformation of a normal farming community into a highly efficient Victorian estate and model village under the management of a titled owner. The Victorians are often credited with the destruction of previous styles and then replace them with that of their own. Undoubtedly some buildings at Thorney were demolished but the result satisfies the wanderer's eyes. Here architects resurrected the niceties of the Jacobean style and blended it with existing buildings enriched with materials from the monastery. The geographical situation of the village, encompassed by some of the best land in the country, helped the radical development of

Thorney viewed from the north c. 1840

what partly remains an agriculturally motivated community. Since about 1880 when the Fens were adjudged entirely drained Thorney was increasingly encompassed by vast expanses of low-lying virile peat soil producing considerable quantities of cereal, potato, sugar beet and other crops.

When the ninth Duke of Bedford inherited Thorney estate he planned to transform the village into a dignified aspect of a well-managed enterprise with practically every amenity then available. He was mindful of his illustrious ancestor Francis, chief promoter of the mammoth "impossible" drainage scheme and his successors all of whom strongly upheld family tradition, sometimes against the inherited views of landed gentry. When the drainage of the Fens was virtually completed and Whittlesey mere sucked into oblivion the Duke embarked on a policy of social and economic reform. He knew that if he was to succeed in what was seen as an experiment attended by risks he must have the backing of a reliable, industrious and contented workforce. The vision gave him no rest and he determined to turn the community into a model village with emphasis placed on practical benefits to the inhabitants. Furthermore he wanted the village to be seen as a community with outstanding architectural aspects and hygienic practices, a place that would be instantly recognised as a model of dignity and sense of purpose, the workers with fair wages which must, to the Duke's way of thinking, minimise crime. The village would be in keeping with Victorian values but this would be tempered with elegance of pseudo-Jacobean buildings to harmonise with the village's older stone faced buildings. As a result Thorney was hailed as a masterpiece, a true manorial estate with precise clean-cut detail to emphasise the achievements of the progressive Victorian age linked with delicate architectural influence which had enveloped the country, especially the cities, in the flamboyant age of James the First. The Duke's architects even added a hint of Dutch involvement as befits the influence of Cornelius Vermuyden, master designer of the general scheme to drain the Fens. Vermuyden has no monument lauding his expertise in the Fens which is a pity, but we see a vestige of recognition to the man in the myriad of drains and rivers visible in the vast expanse of fen.

A the beginning of the 19th century Thorney estate comprised not less than 20,000 acres and produced an average profit of £10,000. Towards the end of the century profit was barely £5,000, this due to a succession of bad seasons and crippling taxation. It says something for the House of Russell when considering that between 1850 and 1912 not once did the titled landlord evict a tenant and Thorney enjoyed the enviable reputation of a healthy community with a minimum rate of crime and no pauperism. This contrasted sharply with the rest of the Fens where the labouring classes eked out an existence in woeful circumstances, families living in squalid tenancies hardly worthy of being called hovels, bringing up families on a pittance, the general picture beyond our comprehension. The Duke was not admired by other landowners who were generally against any vestige of social reform and who argued that the working class should have only minimal knowledge at their disposal and that enthusiasm be strongly discouraged except at work, for, as any master pointed out, "knowledge is a dangerous thing". The Thorney cxperiment was seen as a direct interference with what was then acceptable working practice amounting to a life-time of serfdom for the under-privileged and near tyrranical oppressiveness by landowners. Anything better for the working man and his family was viewed with abhorrence among the gentry and upheld by Parliament on the grounds that "experiments" to the contrary fueled discontent among ordinary people. Britain was gripped by an uncaring social attitude and it particularly barbed the son of the soil. The attitude had descended from the baronial days of the fuedal ages and was largely responsible for uprisings of the working classes, exemplified in the struggles of the Dorchester Martyrs in thcir bid to live decently and with dignity.

The Duke of Bedford was interested in the differences between the classes and he wanted to obtain the best terms for working men and women. He and Lord Shaftesbury acted in direct contrast to the repressive attitudes of Parliament headed by Sir Robert Peel. The 7th Earl of Shaftesbury, an austere evangelical, humanitarian reformer in Victorian England, was noted for his arguments to abolish the practice of using children for sweeping chimneys and encouraging better housing for the poor, as well as enlisting sympathy for young criminals. From the local standpoint the Duke of Bedford perfectly mirrored these attitudes and came as near as any man to the ideal of a wealthy landowner who understood the economics of agriculture related to a happy workforce comfortably housed and which responded with unwavering loyalty.

The Duke was a master in the practice of husbandry and entrenched his ideals within the community at Thorney which could boast pure water, hygiene, good accommodation, a fire station, allotments for tenants, a library and a school. He deemed it necessary his tenants be aware of what was happening in the outside world and provided a community centre and lecture hall. The cottages each had a water tap supplied by a beam engine in the Tank Tower which could be reversed to work a system by which effluent was drawn from the cottages, tanked and sprayed onto the fields. G. M. Young in his book "Victorian England" (1937) surmised that the system practiced at Thorney "was the most successful experiment in social organisation that England has so far seen". To earn such accolade the House of Russell expended almost two million pounds developing the village and estate. It is professionally acknowledged that there is no village in England with a more extensive Victorian display than that seen at Thorney. The munificence of the titled landowner promoted a strong community spirit and I, for one, cannot help but feel admiration for the Duke's ideals and benevolence.

The House of Russell no longer has an interest in Thorney but the spirit engendered by its former heads lives on, epitomised in the cottages and offices and the social contributions portrayed in the buildings in the vicinity of the abbey church. The terraced cottages were leased in direct weekly tenancies, thereby avoiding the drawback of tied habitations. The Duke was appalled at the state of affairs existing in the country's working communities which had been brought to the attention of the aristocracy by Robert Owen, Welsh social reformer who, unlike Lord Shaftesbury, was an experienced industrialist. Owen believed that the environment conditioned character and therefore tried to make working conditions as pleasant as possible. He banned employment of young children and provided them with adequate schooling. He was in fact several generations ahead of his time and encouraged utopian settlements on communistic lines. A natural champion of the Tolpuddle Martyrs in 1834 Owen was connected to various schemes including the Grand National Consolidated Trade Union and his views were sympathetically considered by various countries including America and Russia but turned down because they were too near Socialism for their liking.

A well read aristocrat, the Duke of Bedford was well versed with Owen's writings and he went some distance to build on his early experiments at Thorney guided by Owen's ideal of reform. The Duke properly ascribed to the view that workers should have their dignity, amenities, wholesome and varied food, good homes with bathrooms and be happy and industrious at their tasks. To his mind it was wrong that working men and their families be deliberately deprived of knowledge and higher levels of education. They should benefit from the facility of extra study, something which the ruling classes generally condemned. His enlightened mind came to realise that poverty was not the true order of things. Himself a landowner, the Duke recognised that the problem lay with his contemporaries and went to great lengths to initiate his social experiment upon the principle that a good worker was, for most part, a happy one. As far as the tenants were concerned these attitudes paid handsome dividends employment-wise and socially.

If any criteria could be levelled against the scheme it was this: the workforce lived in a regimented environment. Managers delivered too many lectures and it was expected of workers to attend. For a man familiar with the physical tasks involved it was a little too much to expect him to absorb knowledge approaching academic level. The Duke desired his workforce to be knowledgeable and regarded the Bedford system as a step forward in the improvement of the working man's lot. Certainly the community at Thorney was grateful to their beneficiary for provision of decent homes, fair wages and rents and the means to provide children with a sound education. The Duke had a river cut from the Dog-in-a-Doublet to Thorney and water pumped into the Tank complex where it was filtered and induced into the estate cottages by a beam engine. The cottages even had a bathroom for farm labourers and their families - sheer luxury at the end of a hard day's work.

Ascending the Tank Tower overlooking the village, I marvelled at the complex of administrative offices at ground level which form a restangular shape, the central area built as a stepped reservoir to collect water from the roofs. Hundreds of thousand bricks were used to build an underground reservoir to store water from the river. All this served to promote Thorney as an example of what could be achieved through orderly management, a hygienic environment and every known amenity for workers and their families. As far as the estate workers were concerned the cost of the project justified itself. It gave satisfaction to the House of Russell, but as is often inevitable in many social experiments, increasing inflation and crippling taxation eventually wrote finis to the scheme. In 1912 after about sixty years the estate was split up and sold in lots. For his pains the Duke suffered criticism from his contemporaries and made enemies among Fen farmers whose workers would have sacrificed an arm to work for the titled landowner.

The Duke of Bedford produced a book in 1897, a year said to be a yardstick in the estate's decline. "The Story of a Great Agricultural Estate" declared the position of the enterprise and its management under the direction of one of the largest landowners in the country. Perusing its pages one realises that under the Duke's guidance the labourer's lot had vastly improved and that taxation locally and imperially had increased. The rent had disappeared not only at Thorney but also at the Duke's other estates at Buckingham and Woburn. The penalties in possessing these very considerable estates had become a ponderous burden.

In the period between 1816 and 1895 taxation as regards Thorney estate amounted to £614,714 and successive members of the House of Russell spent £983,640 on laying out the estate and perfecting the productiveness of the land which had been reclaimed by an ancestor at a cost of £100,000, not inconsiderable amounts at the time. Taxation paid over a period of eighty years amounted to nine-tenths of the net income and in 1895 £8,568 was paid in general taxation, leaving a deficit of £441 on the year's working. These figures may not seem much by today's standards but a hundred years ago they were peculiarly significent.

Summing up, the Duke of Bedford wrote: "As to the pleasure to be derived from the ownership of an estate like Thorney, if the reader conjures up a beautiful mansion and park with endless game preserves he is mistaken. They do not exist. The only pleasure which I and my forefathers can have derived from Thorney is the kindly feeling which has existed between us and our tenants and the inhabitants of Thorney town. It was no doubt a pleasure to my predecessors to evolve a pretty village out of the dreary wastes of fens, to create a charming river with well-wooded banks and to make life less malarious and less miserable by a complete water drainage and sewer system, the latter worked by steam. They have their reward in the excellence of the health of Thorney, in the practical disappearance of crime and in the extinction of pauperism. But the economic critic is right in his retort that results do not show a pecuniary profit".

The writing was on the wall. With the sale of the estate an epic chapter at Thorney ended. Wandering around the village one senses the importance of those days when working people elsewhere in the Fens and indeed on the upland regions of the country, eked out a miserable existence in the struggle to live. Thorney must have seemed like a paradise. As the 20th century emerged this laudable experiment in agricultural and social reform drifted into the mists of time to join so much of Thorney's fascinating and rich history woven into the evocative embroidery of great events in the evolvement of Great Britain. But it did not entirely vanish and time bequeathed to the inhabitants as well as to the Fens a rich heritage of architectural magnificence almost without peer - truly the delight of the wondering wanderer.

With the unusual development of Thorney in mind, we might wander from that model village into the outlying grounds of former marsh. Here and there the ground rises on what was formerly islands, most inhabited from Anglo-Saxon times. These became Ely, Wisbech, Chatteris, Whittlesey, Littleport, Little Downham, Coates and March and all periodically suffered from deadly visitations as did Thorney before its titled estate was formed. The Russell miracle ended at the boundary between March and Thorney and the comparison between the two communities was unbelievable. In the towns and adjacent fen surrounding these places all else sunk to a squalid level of existence. Crime was rife and a high rate of pauperism ensured that ordinary working class families suffered from undernourishment and were prone to disease. Hygiene was virtually non-existent and, as a result of neglect mainly by council authorities, the mortality rate increased to astonishing and unacceptable proportions. For most Fen towns the period between 1838 and 1848 was memorable for devastating visitations by diseases of the worst kind, but at March between 1849 and 1850 pestilential out-breaks mirrored the previous bad period except that this was very much worse. The previous years seemed to be a staging point leading to the final, devastating onslaught. Four hundred and forty one inhabitants were carried to the grave and March was relegated as having the worst incidence of deaths per head of population in the country. It was indeed

A typical town court of the 19th century

Little London, March, comprised motley buildings and dark passageways. Interiors were cramped and airless and rooms let out to workmen from depressed areas of the country. They obtained work on farms in the surrounding fens.

a tragedy and alarm bells rang at Government levels forcing a radical change in the management of the town.

Modernday March gives no indication of the squalor attending it in the mid-19th century. I have lived in the town for 50 years, first coming here when my father accepted a post as a shunter at the railway marshalling yards. In those days the town was known as "Smoky March", a grey/blue haze tending to hang over the roofs from the railway where dozens of steam locomotives were regularly fired up in preparation for the day's work. Even then, in the 'forties, my father was told he was going to a place where hundreds of people had died, alluding to the sad events ninety years before when March inhabitants living in riverside cottages and in dismal courts were subjected to the ravages of cholera and typhoid and related illnesses. One of the worst areas, Little London, a conglomeration of cramped houses and cottages which occupied the existing site of the town's main car park, perfectly mirrored unsavoury scenes akin to Charles Dickens' Victorian London.

Wandering the roads and lanes of March as the millenium approaches, one acknowledges the progress the town has made in the

Interior of rural cottage c. 1850 T. Bevis

last century primarily with the advent of the railway centre and the honour of being the County Town of the former Isle of Ely. I have on many occasions wandered along the riverside lanes which give the lie to March's position in the Fens, admiring the cottage gardens, trees and bushes, rustic walls with hollyhocks and ivy and, in the spring and summer an abundance of bird song. The green sward sweeps the park towards the swimming pool and the path alongside the river on the opposite bank affords splendid views of West End and longboats and cruisers tied up at moorings.

A hundred and fifty years ago this part of March was at the centre of the indescribable horror which descended upon the town, the relentless visitation entering almost every home, in some of which whole families died. It was a time when the industrial revolution gathered pace through the introduction of steam power in almost every aspect of industry and scythed through the ranks of working men and women depriving them of jobs much as is being experienced now through the onslaught of new technology. Hundreds of men traversed the country looking for work and many were attracted to the Fens, the area poised on the threshold of huge developments in agriculture and horticulture. Men from the power mills and steel plants elected to live in towns like March or on the farms where they learned new manual skills and searched for rented premises in which to accommodate their families.

March had plenty of speculators and many, with an eye to accumulating profit, built ramshackle places with rooms only four feet high, some without windows to accommodate workers drawn to the Klondyke fields of black gold. Instead of seizing opportunities inspired by the increasing population March, through a mixture of avarice, apathy and neglect, plunged headlong into squalor and debauchery of the worst kind. Despite the benefit of the railway and gas plant, the town became a hot-bed of disease and, helped by the council's reluctance to spend capital on improvements, a piped water supply for instance, March descended headlong into an abyss introducing death and hurt of the most horrifying proportions to the population, no fewer than seventy inhabitants dying from cholera in a single vicious spell.

For almost a decade in the 19th century March tolerated increasing assaults by diseases brought about by lack of hygiene and contaminated drinking water. This culminated in the period between 1849 and 1850 with a mortality rate amounting to plague proportions. Over a long period of time the necessary drainage requirements at March barely existed, though to be fair a similar state of affairs existed in neighbouring Fen towns as well, but March bore the brunt of it. The town might as well have been built on a cess-pit and was rendered more prone to disease by the local authorities' lack of activity and the fact that there were too many over-crowded, dilapidated tenements in use. The mid-19th century was the worst period in March's very long history, at least as long as that of Thorney. Compared to the grandiose achievements of the latter place at the same period March was exactly the opposite and portrayed a highly depressed community literally struggling for survival in what is sometimes described an inspired era, in reality one in which extremes of wealth and poverty made mockery of the so-called enlightenment introduced by the industrial revolution which, if anything, forced the classes farther apart.

Practically all towns in the Fens experienced appalling problems which encouraged periodical outbreaks of disease and large numbers of people died from cholera and typhoid. Much of this centred on inefficient drainage and absence of clean fresh water, communities relying on supplies of wells sunk in typical Victorian courts. These wells were usually contaminated by the close proximity of cess-pits and the main wells in March, four in all, were similarly affected, one situated near the graveyard of St. Wendreda's church. River water was also used and into that was thrown household waste and animal remains from nearby

The Market Place, March, prior to 1900

slaughter houses, the river choked with filth and more often than not stagnant, the fens beyond not at such a low level as now and the run of the river quite inadequate to assist the numerous dykes which drained into it.

Conceived over a long period of time the "system" of drainage at March had transformed the town into a labyrinth of islets and the community was intersected by numerous stagnant dykes supposed to drain into the Hythe, an open sewer running parallel to High Street, into which night soil was deposited daily. The river, too, received all manner of refuse. Ramshackle toilets had been erected above many dykes, some serving as many as a dozen cottages. In the town centre the larger houses had their own cesspits but many of the small, clay-floored cottages had none except that which was shared. Every morning women with yolks upon their shoulders could be seen walking with buckets to the dykes and the river. Insanitary conditions to which stagnant water contributed enormously and cramped, stifled living accommodation

People living in cottages near March riverside were sorely afflicted by outbreaks of cholera and typhoid

together with elected men's unwillingness to improve conditions and avaricious landlords forced an infamous reputation upon March which was nothing less than an insult to its hardworking, beleaguered inhabitants. Indulging in opium was common in the fens and relieved depression born of the wet and malarial environment, but at March that malady took on a different and sinister meaning.

It required a telling report to the General Board of Health to urgently promote necessary and immediate measures for the relief of townspeople. Following the disclosure of the tragedy which had befallen March, the government introduced guide lines based on the results of inspections in all aspects of the town. These were published and sent to other places in the country. The uncaring attitude of local authority was tempered with gracious acts by the few who entered affected residences and tended to the wants of the poor. The Rector of Doddington made regular journies delivering blankets and food to the hovels of the stricken and ministered to the sick and dying.

Most premises were unfit for human habitation and were hemmed in by obnoxious dykes. There was no clean water to wash skin and clothes, and bedrooms were too low and ill-ventilated. There were numerous lodging houses of even worse reputation harbouring filth, disease and crime. Wealthy, well fed residents were not let off lightly either and were heavily taxed for the supposed maintainance of the community. It was obligatory for them to supply bread and flour to the impoverished and support widows and orphans but this requirement was often neglected. Financial anxiety was understandable as the majority of the population was without work, too ill, and excused altogether from any share in supporting the community. March was at rock bottom and drowning in its own mire.

To obtain good clear water was of prime importance and this was found in disused gravel pits covering fifteen acres near Norwoodside. These were replenished by water from two thousand acres nearby. The water supply had to be equal to twenty gallons per day for each inhabitant as well as beng adequate for surface cleansing and the extinguishing of fires. A building was erected to accommodate a steam engine and an iron conduit laid on with street mains, service pipes and fire plugs for a cost of £5,305.

The yearly working cost to install drains to every home and one from the pump connected to the street drains and to pay the engine man who received £35 per annum and fuel for the engine at £72, also to include a pumping well, amounted to about £3,630. Income for drainage came from one thousand and fifty habitations but there was a spin-off from this. The Duke of Bedford had installed an earlier system to draw sewage and apply it to his fields. Fen farmers had not yet realised the value and had no practical experience of application of liquid manures on agricultural land. It was particularly good for grass. Stagnant refuse caused disease, yet it could be economically and beneficially used to feed plants and earn profit for towns. The woeful experience of March helped to bring things to a head at many places in the country and the Act which followed rightly declared "The present condition of Little London (at March) and its deplorable roads and the great majority of court yards ought not to be tolerated in a civilised society".

A first improvement was to enclose the notorious Hythe with bricks and use it as an ordinary drain discharging into the river. Part of this ancient waterway can be seen through the east basement wall of the Centenary church. The local gas works contributed to the repair of roads, gas tar mixed with coal, ashes or gravel and lime then spread on a thick bed of hardcore. It was correctly conceived that if March was to have impervious pavements in its streets and courts, a proper water supply and an efficient drainage system, the improved surface cleansing of the town would result. A workman could attach a hose onto a fire

Residents in these cottages opposite St. Wendreda's churchyard relied on drinking water from a nearby well

plug and direct jets at the filth, forcing it into underground drains. On the whole the improvement to March was achieved at a charge of a halfpenny a week for every house in the town. Cholera had exhausted space in the graveyard and as there were several residences in the vicinity of St. Wendreda's church no grave containing a body of a cholera victim was allowed to be opened unless at a depth of five feet human remains would not be disturbed for fear of contaminating the living. When the new burial ground opposite the church had ben filled an additional burial ground was acquired and interments continued there until the human remains in the first had perfectly decayed. I remember a row of little headstones in the churchyard with initials and dates relevant to the deceased and showing a large capital "C" depicting cholera. It was unfortunate that when the churchyard was cleared not one of these historic headstones survived.

The recommendations offered a life-line to March and gave the community every reasonable opportunity to extricate itself from the unspeakable squalor which engulfed it. Even so it was several years before the town could be described as wholesome and respectable. Records tend to be lenient towards property owners with indifferent attitudes and who had no intention to combat the squalor which they helped to generate. The outlook of the town fathers left much to be desired, they being loath to commit themselves to tackling the problem until they were forced by better men and the embarrassingly prone forms of hundreds of March dead.

CHAPTER FIVE

Whittlesey Mere was the largest freshwater lake in southern England

THE area around Holme is a good place to wander if only for a picnic in its wood, a remnant of an old forest. The village has a fragment of an ancient cross where visiting monks from Sawtry, Peterborough and Ramsey may well have treated the residents' ears to the merits of being more generous to those respective religious houses. Or, should the occasional preaching friar call in they might expect a session of hot gospelling - fire and brimstone stuff - at the expense of the monasteries which owned most of the land and fen around the village.

A charming 17th century cottage with Dutch gables is not out of place for, after all, the great expanse of fens was drained in accordance with a scheme devised by that visionary Dutchman, Sir Cornelius Vermuyden, a highly skilled land drainage engineer. If I had lived here a hundred-and-fifty years ago I could have gazed over Denton Fen and be willingly bewitched by the sparkling expanse of Whittlesey Mere, the

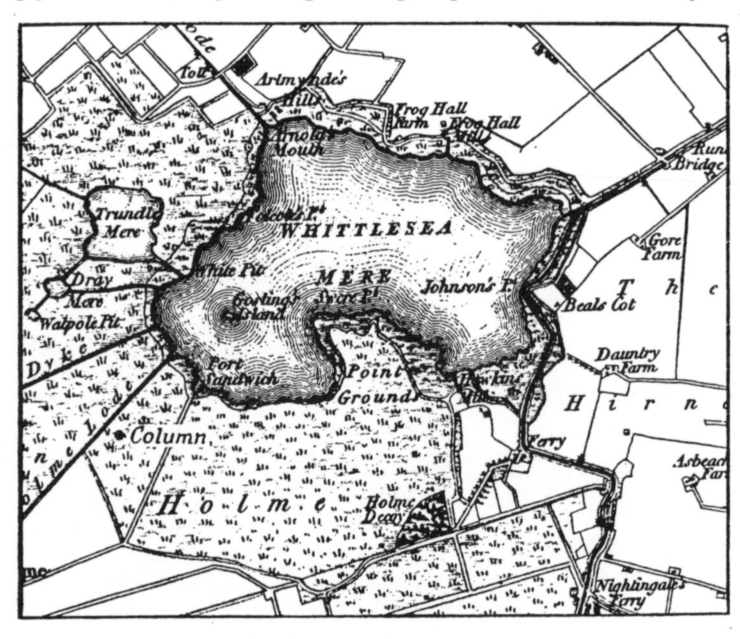

largest freshwater lake in southern England. Or maybe if I were rich enough, join in the exhilarating sport of sailing on the mere with lords, bishops and landed gentry. Perhaps even make acquaintance with Lord Orford, the "Admiral" of a fleet of boats who liked to sail along the Fen rivers making notes about the so-called "ugly women" that lined the river banks as he and his entourage made their way to Whittlesey Mere to take part in regattas and general festivities, with decks stacked with food and more than enough to drink. Wishful thinking indeed! More than likely my lot in life would be that of a Fen fisherman or wildfowler instinctively swatting at pesky gnats or, if I rejoiced in having a small business, paddle my punt with its huge gun and let fly at ducks, taking as many as a score with a single blast of buckshot. Then again I might have donned a pair of long Fen skates and with a sizeable sickle over my shoulder attack the forest of sedge and sell it for crusts of bread.

Enough! The vision of what might have been vanishes and I see now the wide expanse of ultra rich peat fen stretching from horizon to horizon, intersected with dykes and gently waving reeds, a tractor or two snarling away and starlings in quick flight. In Denton Fen instead of billowing sails silhouetted against the sunset and sounds of frivolity in the air, I see a solitary iron post from the Great Exhibition at London driven in 1852 twenty-two feet through peat to the underlying clay. The minds behind the wanton destruction of Whittlesey Mere desired to see how the absence of water affected the fen and had the idea of using the post to gauge shrinkage. When it was driven into the ground the top of the post lay along the surface. Nowadays you get a crick in the neck

looking up at it. In 1932 the fen hereabouts had shrunk ten feet, this indicating, that in these parts at any rate the land was losing its rich deposits and sinking twelve inches every ten years. As I write, the post protrudes at least twenty feet above the surface and it hasn't far to go before it falls. A modern invention was responsible for this novel idea, none other than the world's first centrifugal pumping engine which was set up on the edge of the mere and kept going for a great many weeks until the water had disappeared leaving thousands of gasping fish, slithering eels held by the mud and perplexed wildfowl flying overhead unable to make out what had happened. The initiators of this scheme came in for a lot of stick and in my opinion they deserved it. They could take it, however, as in their minds they had visions of cartloads of money growing in the fields where wildfowlers, fishers and sailing men were at their happiest. In our times it wouldn't be allowed to happen.

What a shame that this old mere which had existed from about 500 A.D. was obliterated in order to grow more food and make a few people fat, not necessarily literally, but extensively in their pockets. The mere was so alive with living things such as ducks, pike and bream, etc. and dragonflies, butterflies, yes! and the stinging gnats, the bane of gnarled leather featured Fenmen. There were countless species of water-loving beetles and other slippery little things. Botanists, too, were in their element not to mention the experts in biological studies. Grass snakes loved the reed shore and frogs could not have found a better place for courtship. Thank heavens we have Wicken Sedge Fen to wander in and use our imagination when savouring its delights and implant scenes in our minds of long vanished Whittlesey Mere with its environs.

The old mere didn't let go of life easily. Before the drainage engine was fired into action it was necessary to dig dykes around the mere and then embank them to prevent the water pouring back into its rightful place. On one occasion, at least, the level of the mere was seen to be considerably raised. Overnight the pressure of the water in one of the dykes had ruptured the bank and it was very happy to reoccupy its old domain. The scheme was delayed for several weeks but eventually the last drop of water was discharged into the dykes, the engine stopped and the vast empty acreage of wet peat allowed to dry.

Whittlesey Mere was a watery highway of great importance to the abbots of Ramsey, Peterborough and Sawtry. Boatmen rowed monks and goods from one abbey to another and abbots enjoyed fishing rights on certain stretches of the water. Some interesting artifacts emerged from the dried bed of the mere. It must have struck one fenman as a curious thing when he accidently discovered a boat cut from a single oak tree filled with acorns and nuts, but more important lying in the bottom of the vessel a silver censer case from Ramsey abbey. Of course nobody knew what had happened to the boat to make it sink or whether the boatman and passengers, if any, had lost their lives. It went

An old woman sells hot chestnuts on frozen Whittlesey Mere, but it's business as usual for sedge harvesters

with a strange phenomenon that happened occasionally. The Fen meres became inexplicably agitated, water rippling as if it were emulating the distant sea. Apparently the disturbance was bad enough to upset fishing boats and other vessels plying between the shores. It happened even on calm days and no-one has fathomed out what caused it. It is on record that passengers were thrown into the water and drowned, particularly on Ramsey Mere. Some ancients would have it that the angel of death seeing people being carried across the meres, dipped his finger into the water and stirred it vigorously, inflicting havoc upon those about their business in boats. Perhaps that's the explanation as to how the monastery vessel sank with its precious silver censer!

The meres may have had their dangerous side to life but none more so than the residue of slowly drying mud after the water had been drawn away. Many Fenmen must have experienced narrow escapes when they ventured too far onto the hardening mud and found a leg being sucked into the mire beneath. An old story from Doddington had it that a Fenman was seen one evening cautiously feeling his way around a newly drained field. A passer-by intrigued by the man's peculiar stance, stopped and called out to him, asking him what he was doing. Turning slowly the Fenman replied: "There was a horse here this morning!" Some wrote that they saw hats floating on the mud surface and presumed that the owners were somewhere beneath!

More hot chestnuts for sale for workers and skaters enjoying the sport of the Fens. A goat cart waits nearby

By far the most engaging story emerging from Holme, centres around a cottager's son residing in the village, who ventured out on a Sunday morning in February 1851. Whittlesey Mere was literally no more and most of the lake bed was in the early stages of drying out and had crusted over. The boy was employed as a bird scarer at Holme Fen and he made his way towards a field near the reed shore which was a quarter-of-a-mile to half-a-mile thick with sedge fourteen feet high. The reed shore was like a miniature forest and a source of revenue to its proprietors. If anyone ventured into and beyond this natural screen they would be lost to sight and the boy, tiring of his static position in the fen decided to take a closer look at the reeds and the bed of the mere beyond. He forced his way through the sedge and when he came to the site of the mere, advanced a few steps onto the crust which gave the appearance of being solid and safe. A few feet away from the shore the crust suddenly gave way and the boy began to sink into soft mud. He

The Fens were famous for champion ice skaters and Whittlesey Mere was the ideal place to hold skating matches. When frozen over it speeded the harvesters' way, too.

was only a yard from firm ground but quite unable to extricate himself and sank deeper into the mire. When the mud reached his armpits his feet touched solid clay and he began taking stock of his situation. He could hear the clock of Conington church and also the sounds of trains on the Great Northern railway line.

It was a desperate business and the boy repeatedly shouted for help, all to no avail. The evening closed in and it was clear to him that he would remain transfixed in the mud for the night, yet despite the cold and rain the mud somehow insulated him and he kept silent throughout the night to conserve his strength. Next morning the boy heard a couple of labourers shouting in the distance, but by that time the cold had rendered him powerless to respond. Then at 10 a.m. by the Conington clock he heard a man moving about on the other side of the reed bed but the boy was unable to make a sound. The labourer moved away and the lad thought his last hope had gone. Half an hour passed then he heard someone pushing among the reeds and in what can only be attributed to divine inspiration the man's footsteps were guided to the very spot where the boy's head and shoulders and outspread arms protruded above the mud.

With the utmost difficulty the astonished man managed to release the boy and carried him through the reed shore to firm land. He had suffered not less than nineteen hours in his intolerable situation. The lad's deliverer himself lived at Holme and recognised the boy and took him to his surprised parents who thought that their son had gone to the neighbouring village of Sawtry to see his grandmother and that she had kept him for the night. The lad was attended by a surgeon who found him to be healthy enough and he was put to bed. For two days he felt the effect of his frightening experience but the following week went to school apparently none the worse for his adventure.

I have wandered on the foreshore of Grafham Water and tried to imagine what Whittlesey Mere looked like. Grafham Water doesn't really afford a useful comparison; for one thing it is too deep and it gives no impression of a fenny environment. The mere was a natural basin whereas at Grafham practically everything is man made and the lake covers farmsteads, roads and fields entirely submerged by water. Voices were raised to hinder development at Grafham and a hundred-and-fifty-eight years ago influential fenny voices and upland voices, too, decried with one accord the disappearance of Whittlesey Mere and that no more would regattas and leisurely sailing be seen there, and that the Fenland economy would suffer as a consequence. Known in medieval times as White Sea Mere this extensive natural lake was abundantly stocked with numerous species of fish (a 52lb. pike was taken from its waters). The mere had a circumference of twelve miles, was six miles long and three miles broad, formed by a branch of the River Nene and attended by numerous dykes and drains intersecting the area. It covered 1,570 acres. Whittlesey Mere was the angler's paradise and the wildfowler's delight. Scarcely a day passed without the echoing roar and plumes of smoke from Fenmen's puntguns. Loads of sedge and other materials were taken from the mere by barges along the rivers to Fen towns.

In summer a variety of sailing boats and rowing boats graced the mere and took part in colourful regattas watched by crowds lining the shore. Winter was no exception, for when Jack Frost had touched the reeds it signalled the time of the Fens' great sporting tradition and skaters in their hundreds appeared on the huge expanse of ice. There was no better place for speed skaters and while they enjoyed their sport other skaters pulled sledges loaded with sedge to gathering points by the shore. Old women, too, took advantage of the hoar frosts and, anxious to earn a shilling or two, sold hot chestnuts to skaters, workers and onlookers.

The mere was mentioned as early as 664 AD when it was granted by Wulphere, King of Mercia, to the newly founded abbey at Medehamstede (Peterborough). The Doomsday Book reveals that the abbot of Ramsey had a boatsgate in his own right, also a second boatsgate held jointly

Barges loaded with sedge and reed from Whittlesey Mere used the rivers and drains and cargoes were taken to nearby towns

with the abbot of Thorney together with two fisheries and a virgate of land. In 1507 Henry VII granted the office of Keeper of the Swannery of the mere to David Cecil for seven years and in 1662 Charles II granted to Edward Earl of Sandwich office of the Master of the Swans within the kingdom and the office of Bailey of Whittlesey Mere. The lord of the Manor enforced strict penalties concerning fishing in the mere and possessed the right to summon fishermen on "fenny ferries" to his two courts held at Holme, and bailiffs proved the nets with a brazen mesh pin. If these were found undersize the Lord of the Manor imposed a fine on the offender and his nets were destroyed.

Dotted around the mere were several wind engines, their sails turning great wheels with paddles forcing water along the drains and into the River Nene and mere. The Rev. C. E. Walker, M.A. in his book "Records of a Fen Parish" wrote lucidly of the windmills seen in the Fen landscape in the 19th century. In his time few of those quaint old-fashioned, picturesque wind engines remained. They were repaired when necessary but never re-built and they were prone to wind and storm damage and very costly to maintain. Steam power, he wrote, was cheaper and more effective "and so an ugly brick engine house with a

Skaters on a Fen drain avoid a sunken boat and a single-wheeled sedge carrier

The Floating Church of the Fens travelled along the Fen rivers and drains and featured prominently in the Whittlesey and Manea areas. Its purpose was that of bringing the message of faith to people living in outlying places, such as isolated homesteads and farms where difficulty existed in attending and communicating with parish churches and their clergy

low chimney which in the winter sends long clouds of smoke across the fen and adds not a little to the dreariness of the landscape, takes the place of the picturesque old-world machine". In Mr. Walker's day you could see the wind-engines on the bank's of Vermuyden's drain one behind the other, gradually receding in the immeasurable distance, with their sails swiftly revolving in the face of the wind. At another time when they were needed, they were becalmed. They stood forty feet high from the base of the tower to the moveable head, every section built of wood. A heavier structure would sink into the soil. Strong winds and lashing rain easily damaged the towers and canvas sails.

On close inspection you could form an adequate idea of the size of the vast sails - thirty-six feet long and six or seven feet broad. Inside, the machinery was simply constructed from a few great beams all of hard, well-seasoned oak and massive cog-wheels. Down the centre of the tower came a beam which, with the aid of a few wheels, caused the huge water-wheel to turn within its huge protective case on the outside. Some of these wheels were thirty feet in diameter, their outer circumference studded with boards which splashed into the water, lifting it from the dykes to the higher river level.

In the winter the mills were occupied by the mill-keeper's family. They lived in the noisy, creaking basement and the children played games such as running out of the entrance and avoiding the sweep of the great sails. The keeper left his cottage and his summer job of roding dykes and took up residence at the mill soon after Michaelmas and he and his family would not leave their post until March or April. The work wasn't easy, especially after heavy rain during "February fill dyke" when water often encroached upon the land almost drowning the young wheat, the wind light and unpredictable. Early in the morning and late at night the keeper had to be ready to work the chain and windlass turning the great head and sails of his mill, or in the event of a damaging gale, get in his canvas. Any reckless handling during the operation could well cause the great sails to "snap off like a carrot" for which he would be called to answer before irate commissioners, "not gentlemen from London, but fen farmers and landlords who knew the nature of things and could distinguish accidents from carelessness right well".

Regretfully not one of these old wind engines survived, the majority being abandoned to decay into the ground. The aspect of them against the open Fenland sky must have been a truly splendid sight. They seemed to be a natural part of the Fens, almost like the remarkable oddity - the Floating Church of the Fens - which travelled along the rivers to isolated homesteads and farms bringing the good news to little congregations assembled beneath its roof. Who knows? It may have stopped alongside a chosen wind engine and the keeper's family and those from nearby windmills gather within the vessel and take communion.

The River Nene linked Whittlesey Mere and its numerous private and ecclesiastical watergates with smaller expanses of water, namely Ugg Mere, Ramsey Mere and Brick Mere owned in the 1830's by William Henry Fellows and a small mere at Yaxley held by Lord Carysfoot. These meres, teeming with life, were vital to the Fen economy with its strength in the regular supply of wildfowl and fish for markets and places well distanced from the Fens. Whittlesey Mere was surveyed in 1777 and the bottom was discovered to be generally even at a depth of four-and-a-half feet. The feasibility of draining it had occupied minds for many years and finally in 1851 after about a year's incessant pumping to a chorus of protests the mere vanished into obscurity.

It was many months before it would bear a man's weight, and cracks and deep fissures spread over the surface which looked rather like the moonscape. In it could be seen the roots of water lilies and other plants. Then along came farmers with horse-drawn ploughs and turned the dried peat, then prepared it for wheat and other crops. Those with imagination will see the mere in their mind's eye as it used to be, a black sea of water fringed with coarse sedge and fat bullrushes with the splendid backing of Holme woods and scrubby patches of primeval forest. The bittern no longer booms, curlews, spoonbills, avocet, ruffs and reeves, tippets and snipe, myriads of butterflies and moths, dragonflies, water beetles, great copper and alder and willow have long since gone.

Can it really be progress when the grand orchestra of wild things, croaking, piping, shrilling, clacking, booming and trilling is ingloriously silenced? Our bellies may gorge with satisfaction the fruits from reclaimed land, but in this instance I believe we are spiritually the poorer.

CHAPTER SIX

Stones of the Marsh - sentinels of the Fens

IN my earlier days I wandered pleasureably and appreciatively around the churches of marsh and fen. Being a bellringer it is hardly surprising that I chose to do that. Obeying the call of the noble art peculiar to this sceptred isle I rang the bells of hundreds of churches and at the same time learned to love the fine towers and spires attached to them. Inevitably my quest took me to the churches of marsh and fen, impassive witnesses of the people's faith in ages past, reflective of their fortitude, courage and determination to make a living out of repeated disasters in the face of the fury of storm and flood. The churches would not let me go and I am still willingly possessed of their charm but more important their story because I desired to gain from a quiet, expectant mind the sobering tranquility of an environment charged with meaning and purpose. Being individuals with different moods and aspirations, when we stand before an old church we should remember that beauty is something definable in many aspects. It is not fixed and absolute, as plain to one man as his fellows. One beholds strong buttressed walls,

traceried windows and graceful pillars and springing arcades supporting the clerestorey bathed in light, and the mind absorbs aspirations from a distant age when men were urged by architectural innovation through one great building period to another.

It is there for those who can see it and feel it, and its realisation is at once the proof and the reward of a certain fineness of vision, of ordered logic of apprehension, the senses of the beholder bridging the centuries, joining the aspirations of the builders. Enter the mind of the man who conceived the plan and realise the miracle of its conception as a tormenting and disquieting vision in the brain of its founder, giving him no rest till he had dazzled his fellows with the glory of the imagination that haunted him, akin to the artist who can visualise the picture on a blank canvas. Then one senses the contagion spreading among the settlers till an exaltation possessed the community and the church, or cathedral, rose skywards emblemising the faith and the promise of greater things beyond this troubled veil.

Here, embodied in our ancient churches is the story of the

discovery of stone as a noble and abiding material; of builders' tenacious grappling with the problems and wringing from the conflict within their minds new discoveries of beauty, of majesty, of sombreness of strength. Foremost in their aspirations was the undeniable urge to enshrine in a framework of fitting and solemn beauty the spiritual mysteries by which they felt themselves surrounded. The grandeur of our ancient cathedrals and churches reaches deeper than the sensuous enchantment of that first wonderful moment when we stand in awe before a majestic building rising from the green sward, its outline silhouetted against the sky.

Little wonder we sense something even more majestic as we see the mellowed walls, for it has its roots in the spiritual needs of mankind in the history of our civilisation, in the static needs of construction and much more so in the Spirit of God which evolved and flowered in the Gothic arts which are splendidly evidenced in marsh and fen. The tone is set with the vision of the great Fen cathedrals, the mother churches of two dioceses seen from great distances on a hilltop as at Ely, and the sombre grey hulk of Norman influence and solidity powerfully portrayed in the masculine, romansque design of Peterborough cathedral overlooking the waters of the River Nene.

The grey mass of Ely cathedral as seen from the River Ouse

These are imperative studies for those of us who sense something more than the surface glamour of the churches in this green and pleasant land, in the hills and vales and wide reaches of fen and marsh where they stand, majestic foils against what was formerly a drab, malarial background of impenetrable marsh. What promise of grace did our forefathers and pilgrims feel as they saw the great monasteries and churches rising above the misty, watery wilderness? It was something beautiful and inspiring they beheld in the soaring arcades, a vestige of heaven, perhaps, because in the first place passion and aspiration are absorbed by their walls. It plays, undiminished, upon the sensitive soul.

Looking studiously at a church building we might apprehend what manner of men our forefathers were and how they lived in the marsh and fen of unbounded hazards, and acknowledge their hardships and limitations, their capabilities and aspirations, even their thoughts. A cathedral and church is well able to speak to the beholder who learned to pierce the material veil. They absorbed the centuries and are still vital and useful, for is not old wine wholesomest, old pippins toothsomest, old wood burns brightest, old linen wash whitest? One recalls the relevant words written by a knowing sage of old time: "One that hath unnatural disease to be enamoured of old age and loves all things as Dutchmen doe cheese, the better for being mouldy and wormeaten. He will go forty miles to see a saint's well or a ruined abbey".

Peterborough cathedral overlooks wooded banks of the River Nene

It is a thing of greater price that the best of our ancient churches are the work of not this man or that, but of whole communities stung with a vision of the unseen and with a common aspiration to lay hold of it and encapsule it forever in the mediums of stone, timber, lead and glass. How well is this seen in the great churches rising above marsh and fen. Even more remarkable is that they are here at all. Stones and marsh do not mix, yet here is a strange thing. The vast plains have stones in great abundance. Enriched, orderly, symmetrical piles of hewn stone dominating with rare grace villages and the surrounding countryside where the sea and meres once reigned supreme.

Marsh and Fen churches are renowned. Mens aspiration raised them in a geological environment where logical consideration confirms inadvisability to build for fear of subsidence; in places where the land was washed repeatedly by the sea and properties roared upon by unchecked gales. Men, patience tested to the limit, laboured with hope and faith and their prayers went up on the wings of the wind and the sound of the waves beating relentlessly against sea barriers, often breaking through. It was unparalleled defiance and it is visible in our own times. Strength of purpose slumbers amid the solace and grandeur of many enriched fanes perched precariously, as at West Walton, upon silt land and on the solid gravel and clay beds of the Fens.

Like the churches they built, marsh men were hardy and uncompromising but the places they left to succeeding generations speak volumes for the vision that haunted them. Numerous churches, embattled and pinnacled, most with elegant towers and soaring steeples, stretch in a wide arc from Boston to King's Lynn. Irresistible magnets to tantalise wanderers such as myself, who cannot fail but be impressed by Gosberton, for instance, where the past speaks so evocably, or Surfleet with its leaning tower, England's very own Pisa. Whaplode church with long nave and massive arches, or the flamboyant grace seen at Holbeach and dignified serenity at Long Sutton. It is remarkable that many of these churches owe their existence to local products of a bygone age - cheese, wheat, barley, cattle, sturdy horses, wildfowl, fish, geese and fleece so much valued by marsh dwellers and fen men and highly prized by dry footed uplanders. Fen and marsh dwellers were wealthy compared with some and they built churches to accommodate two hundred, even five hundred souls, yet the parishes so scattered as to warrant no more than a hundred faithful worshippers and far less in our own age.

If anyone asked me to recommend a typical marshland church I would be hard put to distinguish one. Could it be Walsoken, the Norman style giving way to Early English, or Tilney All Saints with Norman romansque flair. Gedney perhaps, Terrington St. Clement or the Wiggenhall group of churches, splendid examples of fullness of the flowering of the Gothic arts, medieval interiors filled with light from large traceried windows. Even the church at St. John's, Terrington, of unashamed plainness with Georgian box pews. Its real gem is the attached three storied priest's house, and well he may have needed it when water lapped the step to the porch. One might point out the massive detached campanile at West Walton which causes visitors to halt in their tracks. The elegant spires of Marshland are unmatched landmarks and visible from miles away. Moulton, Holbeach, Spalding and Fleet charm thc wanderer with exuberant style and Long Sutton's lead and timber "pointer" claims the distinction of being the oldest spire of its kind. Other noble, slender spires are seen at Leverington and March but the finest steeple of all in the south Fens is that of St. Mary's church, Whittlesey, adhering strongly to the Northamptonshire tradition.

Visitors to the Fens in search of stark simplicity of line are well advised to compare Guyhirn's little Commonwealth church with plain original Puritan furnishings with the dominating church at Sutton-in-the-Isle set upon a hill overlooking the south Fens. It is surmounted with a remarkable lantern tower, traditional to the Fens. Upwell, too, has such a tower, only smaller, but none as fine as the octagon tower at Ely cathedral, a highly acclaimed 14th century masterpiece. Flamboyant use of timber is not usual in the Fens where, in pre-drainage times woods were practically non-existent. Church roofs are generally old but plain. At Elm, Tilney All Saints and Walsoken the roofs stand out, angel figures adorning them. At the former a little boat was carved into the roof to indicate that the sea often had inflow here and people resorted to them and escaped to safety. Without question the finest church roof of all is that at St. Wendreda's church, March, which boasts a double-hammerbeam ceiling with no less than 120 angel figures the majority of half life size. It is said to be the finest example of its kind, and acclaimed, among many, by the late Sir John Betjeman, poet laureate.

St. Mary's, Whittlesey

I think for sheer magnificence overall, certainly in terms of space and ornamentation Walpole St. Peter church takes the honours. A close or equal contender is St. Clement's church, Terrington, a few miles distant, built like a small cathedral. Walpole St. Peter's is Queen of the

Marsh and well deserves that accolade but by the same token Terrington St.Clement is surely the King. Walpole enriches the surrounding silt plain and captivates the wanderer with undying splendour of the centuries. Here one senses the contagion among the parishioners of old as they watched with pride stonemasons setting up their church upon the marsh. They who seek the unusual will not be disappointed here. The church is enlivened with quaint oddities within and without. The exterior stands to impress and prepares those that approach within with awareness of sanctified holiness, a sense of awe and unstinted admiration. To step inside is to lose track of time and be glad of it.

Time does stand still in this place aglow with light, where the sea once raged destroying an earlier building of which only the tower remains. Most of the fabric and more interestingly, furnishings, remains intact from the day the church was re-consecrated five-and-a-half centuries ago. It felt the despoilers' hands when the over-enthusiastic

St. Wendreda's church at March treasures a highly acclaimed double hammerbeam roof with 120 angel figures and also various saints

The Perpendicular church at Walpole St. Peter, renowned for its raised altar with passageway beneath and magnificent windows

reformers removed images of saints and destroyed them in accordance with the authoritative commands of the newly established Church, a period in our history when much wondrous beauty was lost forever. From the turret stairway on the east corner outside, a distant medieval laugh is heard from the worn figure of a giant burdened with the weight of stone above it. This seldom seen gem probably honours the mythological Marshland giant, Hickathrift.

Whenever I helped to ring the bells at Walpole the aspect above the Jacobean screen from the ringers' gallery never failed to impress. My mind focussed on the spacious nave and extraordinary chancel beyond with its several steps leading to the altar. Gleaming candelabra vies for attention and helps to release emotion absorbed by the walls of St. Peter's over the centuries. All is space, unsullied white space from the light of huge transomed windows which would look well in any of our better known cathedrals. The stepped chancel floor ensures that the altar is raised above everyone and everything and it is a rich blessing indeed which newly wedded couples receive when they view from that high spot this lovely church and faces gathered within on their day of days.

The church is surely without a peer. Think and thank we ought to do when we come to Walpole. "Thynk and thank" is the pearl of advice of a priest of old who loved this place and inscribed the font with this thought. With his demise in mind he invites all that look upon it "Remember Wheton Johannes, sometime parson here". We may visualise the benevolent Dominus Johannes Whetholme, to give him his correct title, with his little Marshland flock walking in procession through the portals of this evocative place, their minds filled with wonder and awe.

No-one would be more grandly familiarised with the living bible and with nature through the medium of stone, timber and space, nor by the flash of lightning, clap of thunder and awesome forays of the sea. The Marshman understood it all. Here, in a humble cottage he first saw the light of day; here was his living and his sufferance and finally his end. In this place they brought him to the font and gave thanks; here he walked with his bride and to this church his sorrowing family carried him and lay him before the altar where he had received bread of life, and succour and hope. His bones mingle with the silt which all around affords wealth and standards beyond his medieval comprehension, and he left to our disorderly age an orderly pile of stones to fire the most insensitive imagination.

Separated by a few fields, neighbouring Walpole St. Andrew's church, sadly redundant, seems insignificant compared with its illustrious namesake. The interior is a revelation, pillars built of soft chalk stone amazingly eroded possibly through salt action as a result of flooding in times past. In these hazardous parts men built huge barriers of earth to keep the sea away from their habitations and dearbought land. Standing anything between twenty and thirty feet high, the embankments made good lookouts for shepherds and herdsmen and it was recorded that women could beckon their husbands fishing from vessels afar off. Shepherds commanded a good, if windy, view of the salt grazings and like most countrymen they possessed the knack of interpreting weather patterns, accordingly making provision for flocks and herds, if possible putting them in shelter.

Walton and Walpole areas were notorious for floods which often happened without warning and constant fear was always present of tides lashed by gales, breaching the barriers then engulfing reclaimed land with loss of life and property. When storm clouds edged in from the sea and the breeze quickened to gale force pounding the barriers, threatening cottages and churches the inhabitants knew only too well what the result could be. If the barriers held against the frightening force of nature in her foulest mood, as soon as the tempest abated men carried shovels and hauled tumbrils filled with soil to affected sites and repaired and strengthened the walls. Most storms passed, leaving minimal damage in their wake and accumulating flotsam and jetsam on the seaward side. Nothing was wasted, foraging parties gathering anything of use deposited by the sea. Once in a while the most terrible innundations occurred and high tides joined forces with ferocious gales and storms.

When this occurred tidal rivers swelled and burst their banks, Walton and Walpole areas receiving the initial surge of uncontrollable movement of water. The sea burst through and carried everything before it and raced unchecked over the reclaimed grounds. This phenomenon was known from Anglo-Saxon times as the Aegar - combination of tide and wind. The creeks on the seaward side and protective dykes running parallel with the barriers filled up and disappeared beneath the raging sea and water levels ran at up to fifteen feet above normal.

The sight of the sea in its utmost fury surely struck fear in the inhabitants who could only take refuge as best they could and watch fissures appearing in the barriers and jets of foaming water cascading over the top, followed by the total collapse of sections. The spuming sea poured through, widening the breach as it did so and the water rushed in all directions over the grazings, demolishing buildings and floating cattle away. Water entered the churches and dwelling places forcing people to take refuge on unaffacted embankments further back. In a few hours the whole of Marshland was inundated by the sea and church towers rising above the deluge marked the sites where the villages stood. Many cottages were damaged beyond repair and churches, even today, suffer from subsidence caused by the inflows of centuries ago, a prime example that at West Walton.

Early in the 17th century the sea barrier on Terrington Marsh, protecting Terrington St. Clement, gave way before a violent sea and many of the village's inhabitants were obliged to take refuge in the commodious church tower which is slightly detached. Their requirements were supplied by boatmen from King's Lynn where the mayor enlisted the support of traders who gave items such as blankets and food. Some churches lucky enough to be built on ridges escaped serious inundation but as I wandered around Marshland it did not require a trained eye to observe the buildings which received undesirable washings all those centuries ago. Salt water seriously eroded soft stone pillars at Walpole St. Andrew's church and at Wisbech salt stains can be traced on the eight-hundred-and-fifty-year-old Norman pillars within the church of St. Peter and St. Paul. The effect of floods is even more dramatic at St. Margaret's church, King's Lynn, where walls have subsided and near the entrance can be seen marks indicating high water.

The oldest lead spire at Long Sutton. Many churches in Marshland were inundated when sea barriers collapsed in the face of gales

The impressively massive campanile at West Walton stands well away from the 13th century church building. Marshland towers and especially the detached tower at Terrington St. Clement were places of refuge when the sea broke through supposedly protective earth embankments.

Silt is highly unstable and several ancient Church towers in Marshland lean from the verticle. The Victorians built churches in the Fens and a prime example of a relativly modern steeple affected by insecure foundations is that at Fridaybridge, where the church is being pulled to the side as the tower tilts. The little Victorian edifice at Christchurch, too, was built on unstable land and had a tower which had to be demolished in order to save the rest of the church building. At Benwick the delightful Victorian church built in the mid-19th century struggled in vain to survive. Surprisingly, it occupied a site much too near the River Nene the proximity of which caused hills and valleys in the churchyard and unsettled the tower foundations, stages above becoming dangerous from the twisting of clay and the tower having to be pulled down. This did not, however, prevent severe cracking of the floors and walls and finally the church, too, was entirely demolished.

Builders of churches in the medieval period first laid down strong timber rafts and poured cement around them, adding fleece and even horsehair, reed and other materials to give flexibility. The huge tower at Boston, Lincs. stands on foundations thirty feet deep and into it mixed liberal quantities of fleece. When this very impressive lantern tower receives the sharp buffeting of gales it actually jumps upon its foundations which give way and then spring back again. I have actually experienced this action when standing near the tower's parapets.

In the Marshland it was usual for builders to erect churches on substantial foundations supported by timber rafts. Since about 1800 many of these churches displayed signs of wear and tear, not so much from the elements as from shifting foundations and deteriorating rafts. Doubtlessly repetitional flooding in times past did not help the situation but the builders, aware of the risk of inundation, introduced some unusual planning in church tower design. The Early English tower at Elm is a good example of strength and incorporates a little angle chamber which could serve as a place for the priest to sleep should the building be cut off by encroaching water. A similar chamber can be seen in the tower at Tilney All Saints, a village anciently beset with inflows. At Long Sutton priests occupied a more comfortable room reached by a newel stairway from near the chancel. The best example of all is seen at Terrington St. John, the church having been built in 1423. Between the tower and the church building masons erected a narrow three-storied structure with chambers and passages, suitable as a study, bed chamber and for storage of victuals. Several parishes in this part of Marshland were served by priests from Terrington St. Clement and King's Lynn. In the event of flooding which could happen without warning, the priest would resort to these suitable, if cold, chambers and await such time for the water to withdraw and unruly elements abate.

Walsoken church merits special interest, being a fine specimen of Transitional Norman, the round-headed pillars giving way to a new style seen in the pointed arch of the chancel. The builders continued with Norman-style treatment and the tower is a good example of Early English work. Angels look down from the roof but they are nowhere as numerous as at March. From the west gallery where ringers practice their ancient art I have looked upon the impressive nave of Norman solidness. It is graced with one of the finest fonts in the country, a basin with the seven sacraments - symbolic of Christian religious ceremonies. The arcades at Walsoken church are equal, perhaps superior to Berkeley in detail and the interior as a whole is about the most elaborate and harmonious piece of early Gothic work to be seen in a parish church. In point size and ornament it surpasses many abbey churches yet it exhibits scarcely any approximation of a minster.

West of the River Nene stands a detached tower at Tydd St. Giles, anciently protected by the sea bank but which occasionally allowed the sea to break through. The church is built in the late Norman and Early English styles and is noted for the incumbency of Nicholas Breakspear of whom it is said introduced Christianity to Norway. He left the marshy regions and became Cardinal, then was elevated to the Pontifical seat as Pope Adrian IV. Nicholas Brealspeare was Britain's sole contribution to the Papacy. Go to Leverington church if you would see a restored medieval Jesse tree silhouetted in a window. The tower has stood here for seven hundred years and obviously withstood water encroachment, the rest of the building, except the chancel, rebuilt in the 15th century. Three miles away, Wisbech St. Mary, at peace amidst the orchards treasures its externally plain 14th century church. The interior is interesting and has lots of artifacts. A more recent addition is the floor brass commemorating a former incumbent. The base of the pillars are thought to be of Norman origin and like many other churches hereabouts indicate a rebuilding period probably as a result of destructive floods.

All the large Fen islands were occupied by early Anglo-Saxon tribes but it was not until after the Norman Conquest that "outpost" chapels were built in the marsh areas dominated by the sea. Several chapels existed in the neighbourhood of Wisbech of which St. Mary's is one, the settlements developing on slightly elevated predominantly silt land. When the area was subjected to former deluges, the protective earth embankments forced by storm lashed sea and also inflows of fresh water from the west, elevated ground became a source of refuge for marsh inhabitants. In such repetitional circumstances it was impossible for people to attend the main churches and it was necessary to erect small chapels in places less likely to be flooded. In this manner, a chapel at Guyhirn and one at Murrow, another at Pigg's Drove and a chapel at a

Imagine the awe of old-time pilgrims standing for the first time at the threshold of Ely cathedral towering above the Fens. Every day modern pilgrims culminate their wanderings with a visit to Ely and catch their breath at the sight of the majestic nave rising like a petrified forest above the tombs of abbots, bishops and sacrists who added their skills to this astonishing mass of romansque structure.

place called Kilhusing were erected for the convenience of the inhabitants. Many such chapels were founded throughout the whole of Marshland and on little islands called cotes used as cattle shelters in the Fens proper, exemplified by the village of Coates and tiny Eldernell, the latter place where a miracle of healing is said to have occurred in ancient times.

Marshland's largest church is at Terrington St. Clement, by sheer grandeur and opulence of detail worthy of a cathedral. It is monarch of these parts, a Perpendicular edifice of impressive length and breadth, cruciform, designed originally to carry a central tower. This was abandoned due to the countrywide onslaught by the Black Death, all building operations being temporarily suspended due to a shortage of skilled workers. After a century had passed it was deemed unwise to add the tower at the crossing and, instead, a detached campanile built slightly north west of the church for fear of encouraging the building to lean over as happened to the Victorian church at Fridaybridge. Newton is no stranger to the sea and it was washed on several occasions, many watery incursions coming from breached banks near Tydd Gote. A church was built at Newton in Norman times by a member of the Colvile family, an army commander under William the Conqueror. A descendant founded a little chantry in the marsh - an odd place for a scholastic foundation in peril of the sea. It was swept away by one of the worst floods in Marshland which occurred in the 13th century when settlements at Mumby Chapel and Dolpoon disappeared beneath the waves.

The church at Emneth, too, felt the force of the sea. Its lofty tower suffered from insecure foundations which caused walls halfway up to buckle. This was remedied by inserting a chain in the thickness of the walls, tightened occasionally by turning a screw coupling which one has to step over when climbing the newel stairway.

"Outwell, Upwell, Well and Welney,
But of all the four Wells there are only three,
That is Outwell, Upwell and Welney.

So goes the old saying. Odd one out is Well or Welle, the attractive stream flowing through the two first mentioned villages. This old waterway gave its name to a 12th century priory and the twin villages, Outwell and Upwell, the outer and upper part of the stream respectively, were also named after it. The villages join and are possibly the longest in England, the navigable waterway defining the ancient boundary between Norfolk and the Isle of Ely. The old rectory at Upwell has kept the church company for almost six hundred years. Unusual galleries inside the church were installed in Georgian times. An octagonal lantern caps the 13th century tower, an elegant feature seen here and there in the

Fens and the water meadows of Northamptonshire. Upwell church and St. Wendreda's church at March share the distinction of being associated with Dorothy Sayers, the internationally renowned novelist who lived nearby. Outwell church is as broad as it is long and stands very close to the watercourse which seems to have no ill-effect upon it. The light interior has a fine alabaster monument honouring Nicholas de Beaupré of Beaupré Hall. This great Tudor mansion built in 1500 fell to rack and ruin in living memory and was demolished. It's a shame that not even its most singularly outstanding feature, the gatehouse built in 1525, despite being in remarkable condition, escaped the attention of the bulldozer.

For myself, fen and marsh, the villages and towns, the churches and the rich absorbing history will always afford much pleasure to one who loves to wander, to muse, to tread in the path of forebears and rediscover their faith and aspirations so enobled in the buildings they left behind. It is a challenge to imagination and perseverance and the rewards are physical, mental and spiritual. It was written that seeing is observing, a way of learning and if we cease to wander we may lose our ability to be thrilled by the oddities and exceptions that give life colour.

I daily witness abundant life in the fens and make unhurried decisions and enjoy the passing show. At the end of a day's wanderings, filled with revelation I ponder the beautiful, the strange and the bizarre.